ONE BALL KNITS

Gifts

20 Stylish Designs Made with a Single Ball,
Skein, Hank, or Spool

Fatema, Khadija, and Hajera Habibur-Rahman

WATSON-GUPTILL PUBLICATIONS

NEW YORK

Gifts of love endure in every heart and mind.
We dedicate this book to our dear parents and to
Mustofa, whose endless love and devotion are great
gifts that have left a lasting impression.

We thank our family, whose gifts of caring and
support are always there, and our friends, whose
gifts of smiles and laughter keep us engaged
and enlightened.

Text, project designs, charts, and schematics copyright © 2010 by Fatema Habibur-Rahman, Khadija Habibur-Rahman, and Hajera Habibur-Rahman

Photographs and knitting illustrations copyright © 2010 by Watson-Guptill Publications

Published in the United States by Watson-Guptill Publications, an imprint of the Crown Publishing Group, a division of Random House, Inc., New York
www.crownpublishing.com

WATSON-GUPTILL is a registered trademark and the WG and Horse designs are registered trademarks of Random House, Inc.

Library of Congress Cataloging-in-Publication Data
Habibur-Rahman, Fatema.
    One ball knits. Gifts : 20 stylish designs made with a single ball, skein, hank, or spool / Fatema, Khadija, and Hajera Habibur-Rahman.
        p. cm.
    Includes bibliographical references and index.
    ISBN 978-0-8230-3324-9 (alk. paper)
    1. Knitting—Patterns. I. Habibur-Rahman, Khadija. II. Habibur-Rahman, Hajera. III. Title. IV. Title: Gifts.
    TT825.H256138 2010
    746.43'2—dc22   2009045471

PRINTED IN CHINA

Design by 3 + Co.

10 9 8 7 6 5 4 3 2 1

First Edition

ACKNOWLEDGMENTS

This book would not be possible without the dedication and contribution of many important individuals.

We would like to thank the team at Watson-Guptill for all their contributions in making this book possible. Special thanks to our executive editor, Joy Aquilino: Working with you has been both an inspiring and a rewarding experience. Thanks to project and technical editors Carrie Cantor and Wendy Preston for their conscientious editing. Thanks to our copyeditor, Elaine Silverstein, for her keen eye in catching any glitches. A whole-hearted thanks goes to photographer Heather Weston for the clear and creative presentation of our projects. Thanks to illustrator Carmen Galiano for the numerous illustrations needed to represent important techniques. Many thanks to 3&Co. for the layout, Abby Weintraub for the clear-cut cover, and to all the other individuals who were instrumental in making this book sensational.

Many thanks to the companies that supplied generously: Tom Ware and Wendy Lacy of Bagworks; Karen Rolstad of Blue Sky Alpacas, Inc.; Donna Yacino of Berroco; Chris Roosien of Briar Rose Fibers; Peggy Wells and Kathy Muhr of Brown Sheep Co.; Jerry Harstein of Clifton Associates Inc.; Susan Druding of Straw into Gold; Veronica Van of Dream in Color Yarn; Susan Festa of Knitting Fever Inc.; Susan Moraca of Kollage Yarns; Michelle Owens of Leather Cord USA; Daniela Barbosa of Lion Brand Yarns; Louet Yarns; Diana McKay and Leslie Taylor of Mountain Colors; Anissa Blackwell of Prym USA Inc.; Rob Delmont of Skacel Collection Inc.; Katherine Cade of South West Trading Company; Doris Erb of Sprinrite LP; Tahki Stacy Charles Inc.; and Dana Jones of Tandy Leather Factory.

And Mohammed, Abdullah, and Aasiya, your contributions can never be forgotten.

CONTENTS

INTRODUCTION

A gift can hold special meaning for the giver as well as for the recipient. As we were growing up, our parents instilled in us an appreciation for the particular importance of bestowing gifts, emphasizing through our traditions that the best method to increase mutual love is through gift-giving. When we received a gift, we learned that it was important to express full appreciation by reciprocating, no matter the value of our return gift.

Our family believes that a handmade gift, because of the time and effort spent to create it, is more precious than a purchased one and that such a gift provides a lasting impression of love and friendship. Whatever the occasion, a handmade gift can bring forth a smile, a tear of gratitude, or a warm embrace from the recipient.

We know how hard it can be to choose the right gift for the right moment. Color, design, and attractiveness are all key ingredients. Keeping all these factors in mind, we three sisters have designed twenty unique gifts, paying particular attention to distinctiveness, whether this comes through detailed stitches, artful embroidery, or color and quality of yarn. If you want to knit a gift with more character than the usual pair of socks or mittens, you may find the Square Elegance Lace Bowl on page 50 or the Spiral-Vine Vase Cover on page 92 to be the perfect solution. Looking for a gift to keep a new baby warm or keep little hands busy? You will find cute knits, such as the Cuddle-Me-Baby Hoodie on page 101 or the A-Is-for-Adorable Blocks and Ball on page 107, for the little loved one in your life.

For those who wish to present an extraordinary gift of appreciation that will bring forth not only smiles but genuine pleasure, the circular Dome Afghan on page 112 or the Cute 'n' Cozy Tea Cozy on page 70 may be just the thing. However, if you are a more traditional gift-giver who is determined to knit your loved one a pair of socks or gloves, we have included Little Red Driving Gloves, inlaid with deerskin leather trim, on page 96, and Step-Forward Knee-High Socks, knitted toe up, on page 116.

Not only are these twenty designer one-ball gifts easy to make, each also has an heirloom essence that will last for generations to come. Whatever projects you choose to knit, and no matter to whom you present them, you'll be sure to receive a gift greater than the one you gave: the satisfaction of knowing that they came from your heart and hands. We hope you enjoy knitting these projects, and we wish you joy in seeing the delight of those who receive them.

With all our best,

Fatema, Khadija, and Hajera

Photograph by Heather Weston

ONE BALL BASICS

YARN

Yarn is the essential element of any knitting project, and ever-increasing varieties are available today. To help you figure out which one is right for your project, you'll need a basic understanding of the different types. Yarns are classified according to three fiber categories: animal, plant, and synthetic. Animal fibers are derived from the coats of various animals, including sheep (wool), goats (mohair and cashmere), alpacas, rabbits, and even buffalo. Fibers in the plant category include cotton, linen, bamboo, soy, and cellulose-derived fibers such as viscose and rayon. Synthetic fibers, created from man-made materials, include acrylic, nylon, and polyester.

The majority of yarns you'll encounter are sold as hanks, balls, or skeins. Balls and skeins are ready to use as is, but hanks must be wound into balls before you knit. You can do this by hand or by using a ball winder and swift.

Hang on to the label (also called the ball band) that's wrapped around the yarn when you buy it. This lists the yarn's fiber content, the dye lot number, the length of the yarn in yards or meters, care and washing instructions, and any special processing done to the yarn. Most labels also provide the recommended knitting gauge (see pages 12–13) for the yarn and the needle size needed to achieve it.

YARN WEIGHTS

In knitting terms, weight refers to the thickness of the yarn rather than to how much it tips the scale. The thicker the strand of yarn, the fewer stitches you'll knit to the inch; the thinner the strand, the more stitches to an inch. Yarn weights are divided into seven categories: Lace (33–40 stitches over 4 inches), Superfine (27–32 stitches), Fine (23–26 stitches), Light (21–24 stitches), Medium (16–20 stitches), Bulky (12–15 stitches), and Super Bulky (6–11 stitches).

Ball

Skein

Hank

Photographs by Bill Milne

YARN WEIGHT CATEGORIES

Types of yarn in category
Knit gauge range
(St st to 4 inches)
Recommended needle sizes

LACE

Fingering, 10-count crochet thread • 33–40 sts • #000–1/1.5–2.25mm

SUPER FINE

Sock, fingering, baby • 27–32 sts • #1–3/2.25–3.25mm

FINE

Sport, baby • 23–26 sts • #3–5/3.25–3.75mm

LIGHT

DK, light worsted • 21–24 sts • #5–7/3.75–4.5mm

MEDIUM

Worsted, afghan, aran • 16–20 sts • #7–9/4.5–5.5mm

BULKY

Chunky, craft, rug • 12–15 sts • #9–11/5.5–8mm

SUPER BULKY

Bulky, roving • 6–11 sts • #11 and larger/8mm and larger

DYE LOTS

Yarns are dyed in batches, called dye lots. Colors may vary slightly from dye lot to dye lot. To keep the shades in your garment or accessory consistent, you'll want to make certain that all the skeins you purchase for your project have the same dye lot number (you'll find this information on the yarn's ball band, or label). Of course, for all the one-ball projects in this book, dye lot is not a problem.

PLY

Yarn is made by spinning fibers into single strands, or plies. These strands are then twisted together to create a plied yarn. The ply number on the label refers to the number of yarn strands that were twisted together in that particular ball or skein. Two-ply yarns are made by twisting two strands together, 3-ply yarns by twisting three strands together, and so on.

STORAGE

Store your yarn as carefully as you would your clothing. Keep any unused balls, hanks, or skeins in a clean, dust-free area away from direct sunlight, which can cause colors to fade and fibers to break down. Plastic bins with lids, lidded baskets, or zippered canvas sweater bags are all good storage options. You can add

cedar blocks or sachets filled with lavender or rosemary to keep moths away.

YARN SUBSTITUTION

The instructions for each of our designs list the specific yarn used in the project. This is the yarn we recommend you use. If you want to use a different yarn, you can do so, but knit a gauge test swatch to make sure that the substitute yarn will actually match the gauge of the recommended yarn. You should knit a gauge test swatch even if the substitute yarn is the same weight as the recommended yarn. For more information on gauge and how to knit a test swatch, see pages 12–13.

GAUGE

The gauge measurements in our instructions refer to the number of rows and the number of stitches over 4 inches/10 centimeters of knitting. For detailed information about gauge, see pages 12–13.

TOOLS

There are many knitting tools out there that are either essential to successful knitting or that will help make knitting an easier and more rewarding experience. As you develop your skills, you will find more and more ways to take advantage of the wide selection of knitting supplies and accessories available. Here are the tools that you will need for the projects in this book.

KNITTING NEEDLES

The knitting needle is your most essential tool. Needles come in a vast array of sizes and lengths and can be made from aluminum, wood, bamboo, or plastic, among other materials. For those who knit at night, there are needles with illuminated tips. If speed is your goal, nickel-plated needles may be the choice for you. Other knitters prefer the warm feel of wood or bamboo. It is important to pick the right type of needle for your project and one that suits your personal knitting style. Your needles should help, not hinder, your knitting efforts, so try various styles until you find the one that works best for you. Comfort and ease are essential when knitting.

CIRCULAR, DOUBLE-POINTED, AND SINGLE-POINTED NEEDLES

There are many varieties of needles to choose from, each with its own specific use. Straight needles are the most familiar type; they are essentially long sticks with a point at one end and a knob at the other that keeps the stitches from sliding off the needle. They are sold in pairs in a variety of lengths, the two most popular being 10 and 14 inches. A circular needle consists of two straight needles connected by a wire or tube. Circular needles also come in varying lengths. They are most often used for knitting hats, socks, and other items in the round; but many knitters also use them to knit flat pieces. Double-pointed needles are short needles with points at both ends. Sold in sets of four or five, they're most often used for small circular projects, turning sock heels, and making I-cord.

CABLE NEEDLES & STITCH HOLDERS

Cable needles are short needles with points at both ends that are shaped either like a fishhook or the letter *U* to prevent stitches from slipping off the needle as you work a cable. When instructed, you will slip stitches onto the

KNITTING NEEDLE SIZE CHART

U.S. Sizes	Metric Sizes
0	2 mm
1	2.25 mm
2	2.75 mm
3	3.25 mm
4	3.5 mm
5	3.75 mm
6	4 mm
7	4.5 mm
8	5 mm
9	5.5 mm
10	6 mm
10½	6.5 mm
11	8 mm
13	9 mm
15	10 mm
17	12.75 mm
19	15 mm
35	19 mm
50	25 mm

cable needle and hold them to the front or the back of the work as you knit the remaining stitches of the cable.

Stitch holders, which resemble long safety pins, are used to hold open neckline or other stitches that will be bound off or picked up later. They are available in a variety of sizes, but smaller ones are used most often.

STITCH MARKERS

Stitch markers are small plastic or rubber rings used to mark the beginning of a new round in circular knitting or to indicate where to increase, decrease, or change stitch patterns. When the instructions indicate the use of a stitch marker, slip the marker onto your right-hand needle and continue knitting as indicated in the pattern. Yarn shops carry a wide variety of stitch markers, but you can easily create your own by tying a contrasting piece of yarn around your needle at the same place you would position the stitch marker. When you reach the marker, slip it from the left to the right needle so it remains in place in the row or round.

ROW COUNTERS

Row counters are handy little gadgets that help keep track of how many rows of knitting have been completed. Some slip onto knitting needles, while others are hand-held. Turn the knob (or click a button) to advance to the next number every time you complete a row.

POINT PROTECTORS

These little rubber or plastic caps slip over the points of your needles, protecting the tips and keeping stitches from sliding off. They also prevent the needle points from poking through the lining of your knitting bag.

TAPESTRY NEEDLES

These large-eyed needles with blunt or rounded tips are used for seaming, weaving in ends, and embroidering.

TAPE MEASURE

An accurate tape measure is essential for both construction and blocking. Choose a flexible plastic or fiberglass tape marked in both inches and centimeters to accurately measure stitch and gauge as well as the finished size of your knitted pieces.

CROCHET HOOK

A crochet hook is perfect for picking up dropped stitches or attaching fringe. Smaller crochet hooks work best for these purposes.

PINS

Pins are used to hold and shape the knitted fabric pieces during blocking or to pin together pieces for seaming. Any pin will do, but specially designed blocking pins with long shanks and flat heads are both durable and easy to use.

BLOCKING BOARD

For blocking (see page 34), you'll need a flat, padded, and pinnable surface large enough to accommodate a fully flat and smoothed knitted piece. You can purchase a blocking board or simply use a folded towel spread out over a carpet.

SPRAY BOTTLE

If you use the wet blocking method (see page 34), you will need a spray bottle filled with water.

STEAM IRON OR STEAMER

Steam is required during the steam blocking process (see page 34); either a steam iron or a steamer will serve the purpose.

UNDERSTANDING KNITTING INSTRUCTIONS

Knitting instructions have their own vocabulary and terms that are important to understand before you start a project. Here are the knitting terms we use in our instructions.

SKILL LEVEL

We have divided our projects into four different skill levels: Beginner (first-time projects, simple stitches, and minimal shaping), Easy (simple stitches combined with easy stitch changes, color changes, and minimal shaping), Intermediate (a greater variety of stitches, including more complicated lace and cables, double-pointed knitting, color changes, and shaping), and Experienced (advanced knitting techniques, intricate cable and lace stitches, Fair Isle patterns, and shaping). Most of our projects fall under the Beginner and Easy skill levels, but if you're a beginner and feel that you can complete an Intermediate project, go for it.

FINISHED MEASUREMENTS

The finished dimensions of the knitted piece, after blocking and assembling, are provided for each project.

YARN

Instructions specify the type of yarn used for the project and the approximate yardage included in the ball or skein.

MATERIALS

This list gives all the tools and supplies required to knit the project, including the materials we used to knit our samples.

GAUGE

Gauge refers to the number of stitches and rows per inch of knitting, based on the size of a knit stitch. The size of the stitch is determined by the yarn and needle size used, as well as by how a particular knitter holds the yarn. In our knitting instructions, gauge is measured over 4 inches/ 10 centimeters (4"/10cm). If your gauge does not precisely match the gauge given in the instructions, the size of your finished piece will be different. It is therefore essential that you check your gauge by knitting a test swatch before starting each project. Here's an example of how gauge will be stated in our instructions: 16 stitches = 4"/10cm over St st (knit one row, purl next row).

The Gauge Test Swatch

Even if you are using the exact yarn and needles recommended in the instructions, you'll need to knit a test swatch to check the gauge. This is because not every knitter controls the yarn in exactly the same way, and you may get a different number of stitches per 4 inches than another knitter, even if you are both using the exact same yarn and needles. Using a yarn other than the one specified in the pattern will also affect gauge (see Yarn Substitution, page 9). To make the test swatch, use the same needles and yarn you plan to use for the project to cast on the number of stitches required to get at least 4 inches of knitting (usually 20 or more stitches). Knit until you have a swatch that measures at least 4"/10cm square. Flatten the swatch, straighten the rows and stitches, lay the tape measure on top of the swatch, and count the number of stitches and rows as follows.

1. Count the number of stitches across 2"/5cm; multiply the results by 2 to get the number of stitches per 4"/10cm.

2. Count the number of rows along 2"/5cm; multiply the results by 2 to get the number of rows per 4"/10cm.

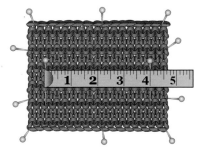

If you find that your gauge does not match the gauge given in the instructions, try changing your needle size. Larger-size needles will decrease the number of stitches per inch; smaller-size needles will increase the number of stitches per inch.

PATTERN NOTES

This section of the instructions explains any important information concerning the project, clarifications of certain instructions, or variations you might try.

COMMONLY USED ABBREVIATIONS

Abbreviations are used in written knitting instructions, and we provide a list of any

*	repeat instructions after or between asterisks across a row or round, as instructed
( )/[ ]	work instructions as a group a specified number of times
beg	beginning
BO	bind off
CO	cast on
cont	continue; continuing
dec	decrease; decreasing
dpn/dpns	double-pointed needle/needles
foll	follow, follows, following
inc	increase/ increasing
k	knit
k2tog	knit 2 together
LH	left-hand
p	purl
p2tog	purl 2 together
patt/patts	pattern/patterns
pm	place marker
psso	pass the slipped stitch over
rep	repeat
RH	right-hand
Rnd/rnd	round
RS	right side
skp	slip one, knit one, pass the slipped stitch over
Sl	slip
Ssk	slip, slip, knit
st	stitch
St st	stockinette stitch
Tbl	through back loop
WS	wrong side
yo	yarn over

special abbreviations used in each project's instructions, along with their meanings. The chart lists some of the most commonly used abbreviations.

STITCH PATTERNS

In most cases, the stitch pattern or patterns used in a project will be presented both as written instructions and in chart form. You will refer to the written instructions and chart(s) when the project instructions call for that specific stitch pattern.

KNITTING INSTRUCTIONS

This is where the knitting instructions for each project begin. We tell you how many stitches to cast on, which stitch pattern to use, how much to knit, and how many stitches to bind off.

CHARTS

In most cases, the written instructions for each stitch pattern are accompanied by charts. These charts are visual representations of the stitch patterns. Many knitters find them easier to follow than the line-by-line written instructions.

How To Read Charts

Each small square, or block, in a chart represents one stitch or one knitting action, such as a knit stitch, an increase, or a decrease. Each chart is accompanied by a legend that explains the meaning of each symbol that appears in the blocks. You'll notice that there are numbers running along both the right- and left-hand sides of the chart. These refer to row numbers; for example, the number 1 refers to Row 1. If the numbering begins on the right-hand side of the chart, you will start knitting on the right side (RS) of the work. When the numbering begins on left-hand side of the chart, you will begin knitting on the wrong side (WS).

Figure 1 shows a chart that begins with a right-side row. Notice that the numbering of rows starts on the right. This indicates that you will begin knitting Row 1 from the right, moving to the left. In this case you will read all odd-numbered rows from right to left and all even-numbered rows from left to right.

The chart in Figure 2 starts with a wrong-side row. In this case you will read all odd-numbered rows from left to right and all even numbered rows from right to left.

Figure 3 shows a chart as it will appear in the instructions, complete with stitch symbols.

Row 1 (RS): Skp, *yo, k1, yo, k3tog, yo, k1; rep from * to last 2 sts, yo, k2tog.
Row 2: Purl.
Row 3: *K4, yo, skp; rep from * to last 3 sts, k3.
Row 4: Knit.

SCHEMATICS

Schematics are line illustrations that show the design, or design piece, laid flat. Schematics are labeled with the name of the piece and the exact measurements that each piece should be when completed.

Figure 1

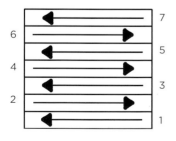

Figure 2

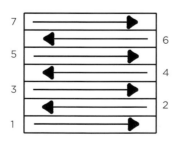

Figure 3

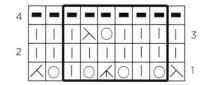

Photograph by Heather Weston

KNITTING TECHNIQUES

MAKING A SLIP KNOT

1. Pull out a length of yarn from the ball and form it into a pretzel as shown.

2. Insert the needle under the bar and pull a loop.

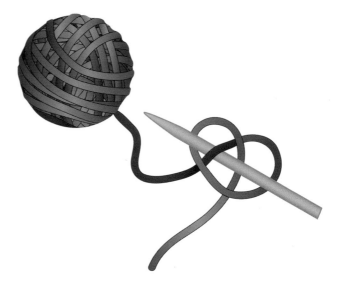

3. Tighten the loop with your thumb and index finger.

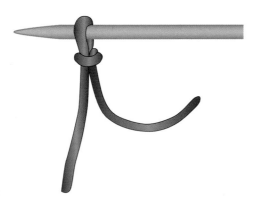

CONTINENTAL LONG-TAIL CAST-ON

1. With the slip knot on the needle, wrap the short end of the yarn around your thumb. Wrap the yarn from the ball around your index finger. Hold both ends of the yarn taut in the palm of your hand.

2. Insert the needle into the loop near the thumb and lift it.

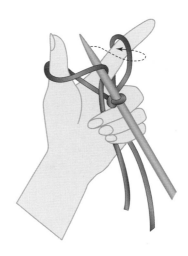

3. Keeping the thumb loop on the needle, slip the needle into the loop from the index finger. Pull a new loop through the thumb loop. One stitch is made.

CABLE CAST-ON

1. With the slip knot on the needle, insert
    the right-hand needle from the front to
    the back of the stitch. Wrap the yarn from
    back to front around the needle.

2. Pull the wrapped yarn through the stitch,
    being sure not to drop the worked stitch
    off the left-hand needle.

3. Slip the stitch from the right-hand needle
    to the left-hand needle. Two stitches are
    on the left-hand needle.

PROVISIONAL CAST-ON

1. With scrap yarn, slip-knot one stitch onto the crochet hook. Place knitting needle between the crochet hook and the working yarn. *Wrap the yarn around the crochet hook, pulling through slip knot on the crochet hook. Make one stitch on the knitting needle. Place the yarn behind the knitting needle. Repeat from * until the correct number of stitches is made per the instructions.

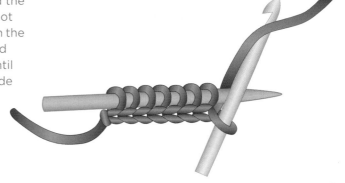

2. *Carefully remove one crochet provisional cast-on stitch by pulling on the scrap yarn. One loose live stitch is made. Insert the right-hand needle into the center of the live stitch. Repeat from * until all live stitches are on the right-hand needle as directed in the pattern. Discard the scrap yarn.

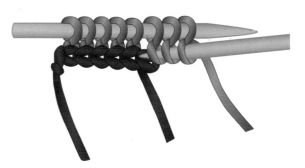

KNIT STITCH

1. Keeping the yarn in back, insert the right-hand needle from the front into the back of the first stitch.

2. Wrap the yarn around the needle from back to front once.

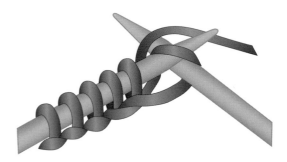

3. Pull the wrapped yarn through the first stitch.

4. Keep the new stitch on the right-hand needle; drop the first stitch from the left-hand needle.

NOTE: When every row is worked in the knit stitch, **garter stitch** is formed. Each ridge, or row of bumps, represents two rows worked. Garter stitch fabric is elastic and holds its shape well.

PURL STITCH

1. Keeping the yarn in front between the two needles, insert the right-hand needle from the back to the front of the first stitch on the left-hand needle. Wrap the yarn around the stitch on the right-hand needle from back to front once.

2. Pull the wrapped yarn through the back.

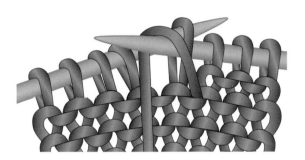

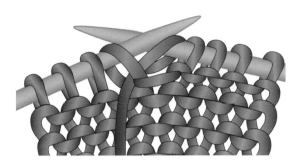

3. Keep the new stitch on the right-hand needle; drop the first stitch from the left-hand needle.

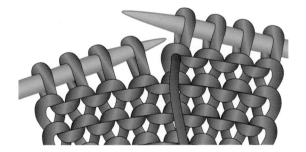

SLIP STITCH KNITWISE

Insert the right-hand needle through the stitch as if to knit. Slide the stitch off the left needle and onto the right needle without working the stitch.

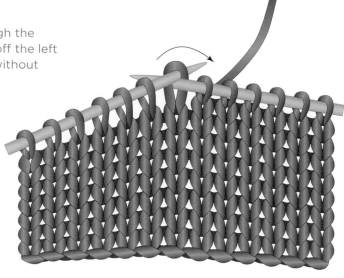

SLIP STITCH PURLWISE

Insert the right-hand needle through the stitch as if to purl. Slide the stitch off the left needle and onto the right needle without working the stitch. Note: The stitch will be twisted.

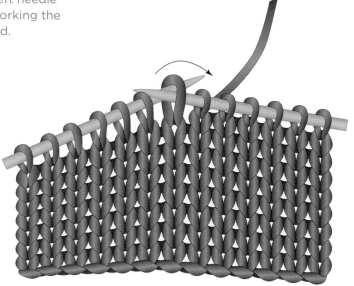

YARN OVER BETWEEN KNIT STITCHES

1. Bring the yarn forward between the two
    needles and lift it over the right-hand
    needle.

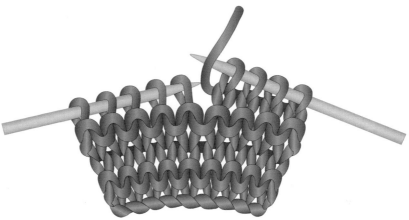

2. Knit the next stitch, bringing the yarn
    to the back over the right needle and
    producing a loop before the knitted stitch.

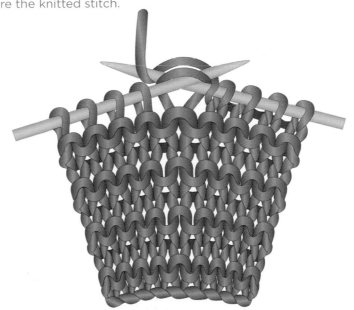

YARN OVER BETWEEN PURL STITCHES

Leave the yarn in the front of the work and wrap it around the right-hand needle once. Purl the next stitch. (See the Purl Stitch instructions on page 21.)

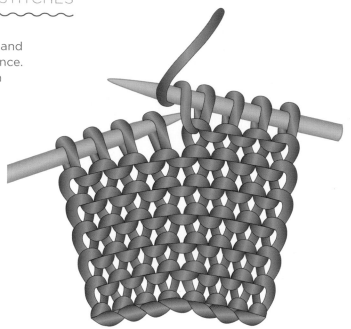

INCREASE (KNITTING INTO THE FRONT AND BACK LOOPS)

1. Knit into the front loop of the stitch without dropping the worked stitch from the left-hand needle.

2. Knit into the back loop of the same stitch. Drop the worked stitch from the left-hand needle. Two stitches are on the right-hand needle.

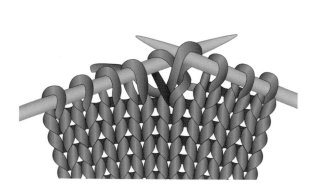

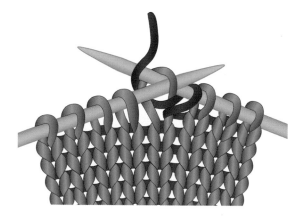

MAKE 1 LEFT INCREASE

1. For a "Make 1 Left" increase, insert the left-hand needle from front to back into the horizontal strand between the last stitch worked and the next stitch on the left-hand needle.

2. Pick up this strand and knit through the back loop.

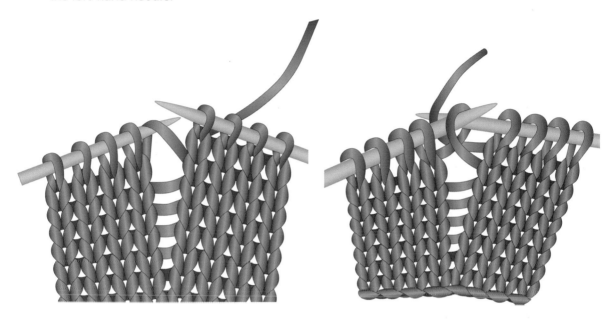

A Make 1 increase can "lean" either right or left. For a "Make 1 Right" increase:
   Insert the left-hand needle from back to front into the horizontal strand between the last stitch worked and the next stitch on the left-hand needle. Pick up this strand and knit through the front loop.

DECREASE (SLIP 1, K1, PSSO, OR SKP)

1. Insert the right-hand needle into the first stitch as if to knit and slip it onto the needle.

2. Knit the next stitch. Pass the slipped stitch over the knit stitch.

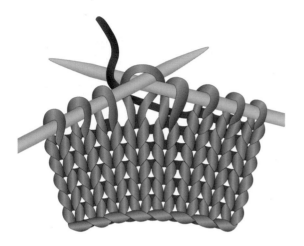

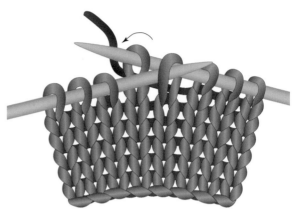

PICKING UP DROPPED STITCHES

Work to the dropped stitch. Using a small crochet hook, insert it into the dropped loop, hooking to the bar above it. Pull the bar through the dropped stitch. Continue to ladder upward by pulling the bar through the stitch below.

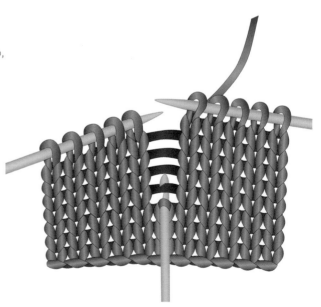

BINDING OFF

Knit 2 stitches. *Insert the left-hand needle into the first knit stitch on the right-hand needle. Lift this stitch over the second stitch and off the needle; repeat from * to the end.

THREE-NEEDLE BIND-OFF

Hold the two pieces to be joined with the right sides of the fabric facing each other and with both needles pointing to the right. Using a third needle of the same size, knit together the first stitch on each needle, as shown. *Work the next stitch on each needle in the same way. You now have two stitches on the right-hand needle. Lift the first stitch over the second stitch and off the needle. Repeat from * to the end.

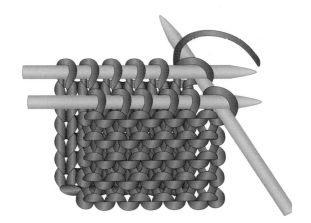

CIRCULAR KNITTING (KNITTING IN THE ROUND)

Cast on a number of stitches. Begin knitting across the stitches on the needle until you reach the last cast-on stitch. Work the last cast-on stitch, and place the marker on the right-hand needle point. Join the round, being careful not to twist the stitches on the needle. Tighten the stitch and proceed with working the next round.

KNITTING WITH DOUBLE-POINTED NEEDLES

1. Cast on a number of stitches on a single-pointed needle. Slip the cast-on stitches evenly onto three or four double-pointed needles.

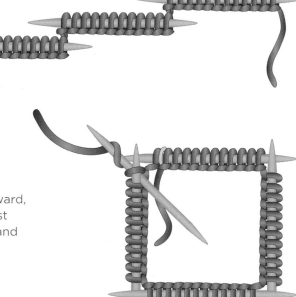

2. With the cast-on edges facing inward, take a free needle and knit the first cast-on stitch. Tighten the stitch and proceed to knit.

KNITTING CABLES

1. Slip three stitches purlwise onto the cable. Hold the cable needle in front of the work.

2. Knit the next three stitches on the left-hand needle, continuing to hold the cable needle in front of the work..

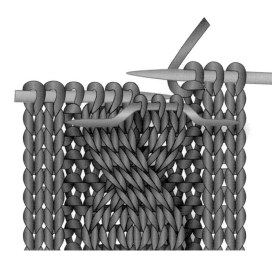

3. Knit the three stitches directly from the cable needle. If it's easier for you, you can return the stitches to the left-hand needle and then knit them. The cable has now been made.

NOTE: These illustrations show how to make a six-stitch front, or left, cable. Follow the specific instructions in your pattern to determine how many stitches are included in the cable. To make a back, or right, cable, follow the same three steps, but hold the cable needle in back of the work instead of in front of it.

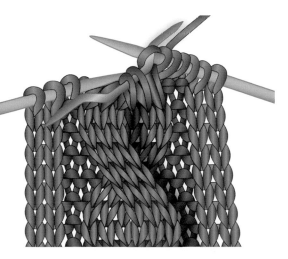

KNITTING I-CORD

Cast on the number of stitches directed in the instructions. *Knit across the cast-on stitches. Without turning the work, slip the stitches back onto the left-hand needle. Repeat from * until you have reached the desired length. Bind off.

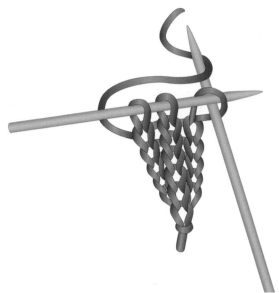

CREATING SHORT ROWS WITH WRAPPED STITCHES

WRAPPING A KNIT STITCH

1. Slip one unworked stitch from the left-hand needle to the right-hand needle purlwise. Bring the yarn forward between the slipped the stitch and the next stitch on the left-hand needle.

2. Return the slipped stitch back to the left-hand needle. Turn the work, keeping the yarn wrapped around the stitch. Work across as directed.

Step 1

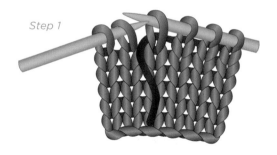

WRAPPING A PURL STITCH

Follow the steps for wrapping a knit stitch except, when wrapping, bring the yarn from front to back between the slipped stitch and the next stitch on the left-hand needle. Turn the work and keep the yarn wrapped around the stitch. Continue to work across as directed.

Step 2

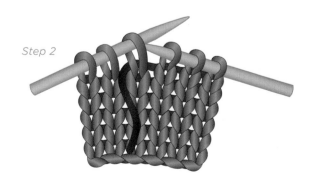

KNITTING A WRAPPED STITCH

Insert the right-hand needle under the wrapped stitch and through the knit stitch, from front to back knitwise. Place the two stitches on the needle. Knit the wrapped stitch and the knit stitch together.

PURLING A WRAPPED STITCH

Insert the right-hand needle under the wrapped stitch and through the purl stitch, from back to front purlwise. Place the two stitches on the needle. Purl the wrapped stitch and the purl stitch together.

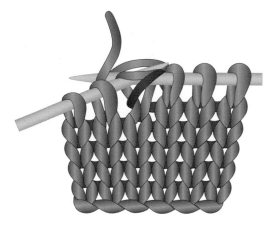 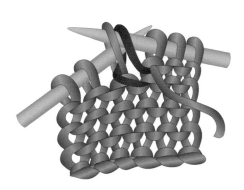

PICKING UP STITCHES ALONG A BOUND-OFF EDGE

1. Working along the bound-off edge, insert the needle through the center of the first stitch. Wrap the yarn around the needle as if to knit.

2. Pull the yarn through the stitch. You have picked up one stitch. Repeat to pick up additional stitches.

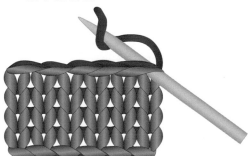 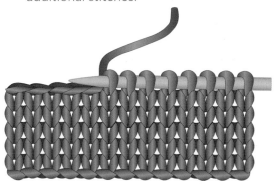

KITCHENER STITCH (GRAFTING)

Before you begin, make sure you have the same number of stitches on both needles, and hold the front needle parallel to the back needle. The yarn that you use to thread the tapestry needle should be attached to the knitting on the back needle.

To set up the grafting sequence: Insert the threaded tapestry needle through the first stitch on the front needle as you would to purl, then through the first stitch on the back needle as if to knit. (The yarn should always remain under the knitting needles.)

*Insert the tapestry needle again through the first stitch on the front needle, this time as you would to knit, then slip it off the needle. Go into the next stitch on the front needle as if to purl, leaving it on the needle.

Insert the tapestry needle through the first stitch on the back needle as if to purl, then slip it off the needle.

Go into the next stitch on the back needle as if to knit, leaving it on the needle.*

Repeat these four steps—front needle, knit, slip off; front needle, purl, leave on; back needle, purl, slip off; back needle, knit, leave on—until one stitch remains, then pull the yarn through the loop.

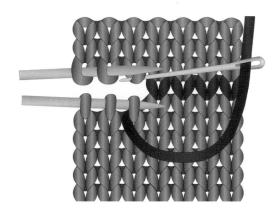

ADDING FRINGE

Follow our easy method for making fringe. Your fringe will always be even in length.

1. Cut out a piece of cardboard, making its width equal to the desired length of the fringe.
2. Wrap the yarn around the cardboard the number of times indicated in the pattern instructions. Cut through the yarn along the bottom edge of the cardboard.
3. Remove the fringe from the cardboard and fold the fringe in half, keeping the bottom edges even.
4. Insert a crochet hook from the back to the front of the knitted piece, then hook it into the center of the folded fringe. Draw the yarn loop through the edge of the garment. Slip the fringe tail through the loop and tug tightly to secure it.

5. Trim the edges of the fringe if necessary.

FINISHING

Properly finishing your project is as vital to a successful outcome as the actual knitting. In this section we give you instructions for felting, blocking, seaming and adding embellishments to your projects.

FELTING

Felting is a process that changes the texture, size, and feel of knitted fabric by altering the fibers so that you can no longer see the individual stitches and rows. It also shrinks the knitted fabric; but it is the fusion of the fibers, not the shrinking, that creates the felted surface. Any fabric made of animal fibers, such as wool, mohair, or cashmere, can be felted.

A fabric that has been felted is thicker, more velvety, and warmer than the original knitted fabric. Felted fabric can be cut and sewn because it won't unravel or lose stitches. Felting works particularly well for appliqués, hats, and bags. It's fun and easy to do, particularly when applied to fabrics knit with big needles (that is, with loose stitches). Felting projects usually instruct you to use needles two or more sizes larger than the yarn label recommends.

Felting is accomplished by subjecting the knitted piece to hot soapy water (which opens up the scales on wool fibers), then agitating the piece to cause the fibers to tangle together. When the piece cools and dries, the scales close up, locking the fiber into thick, durable fabric that won't unravel. Felting can be done with a washing machine or by hand. **Note:** Make sure your knitted edges are finished, that the ends are woven in securely, and that all seams have been stitched before you begin the felting process. Otherwise, you'll create a big mess.

Machine Felting

Felting in the washing machine is the easiest and most reliable method. Place the knitted fabric in a washer using a small amount of hot water and small amount of laundry detergent (no bleach!). Machine wash the knitted fabric along with a denim garment (one that won't bleed) or inside a zipped pillowcase for 7 to 10 minutes. The denim (or pillowcase) creates extra friction, which speeds up the felting process. Check the fabric periodically, before you reach the spin cycle, to see if it has felted. You'll know it's ready when the knitted stitches and rows are no longer visible. Some yarns take longer to felt than others, so don't worry if your fabric hasn't felted within

10 minutes. Just keep it in the wash cycle, repeating the cycle if necessary, and keep checking every few minutes. When the fabric reaches the desired appearance, machine rinse it in cool water and then spin on gentle (never wring the fabric).

Remove the fabric from the washing machine (you will notice that it has shrunk significantly from its original size), lay it flat, and gently straighten and shape it, leaving it to air-dry. Remember that if you don't like your finished result, you can always felt it some more. (You can't, however, unfelt something that has already been felted.)

Hand Felting

Soak knitted fabric in a bowl, sink, or tub filled with hot water for 30 minutes. Add a small amount of laundry detergent to the water and hand wash it, rubbing the fabric together until you reach the desired degree of felting. Rinse the felted fabric under cold water to stop the felting process. Squeeze out the excess water (never wring), and then lay the fabric flat, shape it, and leave it out to air-dry.

BLOCKING

Blocking is an essential step. In blocking, the finished knitted pieces are dampened or steamed and then smoothed into shape, ensuring that the exact measurements for the project are met and that all the rows and stitches are straight and even. There are two methods: wet blocking and steam blocking.

In *wet blocking*, the piece is laid flat on a blocking pad or any padded surface, smoothed, straightened, and pinned down according to the project's finished measurements. Once you are sure the rows and stitches are flat, even, and straight and the measurements are correct, fill a spray bottle with cold water and spray the piece to wet it thoroughly. Leave the piece pinned in place until it is completely dry.

You can also wet the piece before pinning by submerging it in water. Gently squeeze out excess water (do not wring), and then place the piece on your blocking pad and pin it as shown in the illustration below. Allow the piece to dry completely before unpinning.

Steam blocking involves the use of a steam iron. Position the piece and pin it in place as shown in the illustration. Adjust the iron's heat setting according to the fiber content of the yarn used. Hold the iron several inches above the knit fabric when steaming.

Do not allow the iron to touch the knitted fabric. If you do, you may scorch the yarn or flatten the stitches.

SEAMING

We seamed most of the projects in the book using mattress stitch, which gives your fabric a clean, seamless look.

Wet blocking (left) and steam blocking (right)

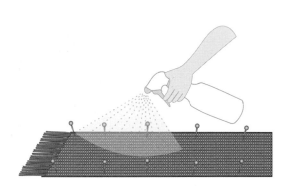
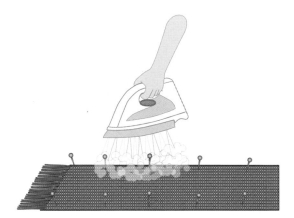

SEAMING AND EMBROIDERY STITCHES

MATTRESS STITCH

Knit side (shown): Place the garment pieces you will be joining side by side on a flat surface with the knit side facing up. Insert the tapestry needle behind the horizontal bar of the knit stitch on the right-side edge of one garment piece. Repeat for the left-side edge of the other garment piece. Continue joining the pieces, stitching left and right edges together.

Purl side: Place the garment pieces to be joined side by side on a flat surface with the purl side facing up. Insert the needle under one horizontal bar of the purl stitch on the right-side edge of one garment piece, then repeat the same for the left-side edge on the other garment piece.

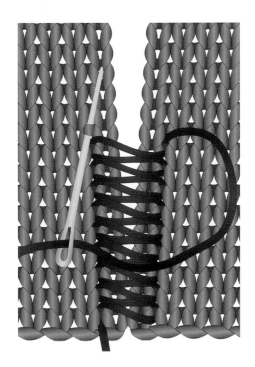

INVISIBLE HORIZONTAL SEAM

With the right sides of the fabric held together so that the stitches are aligned as shown, insert the tapestry needle behind one stitch on one piece of the fabric and then behind one stitch on the other piece. Continue as shown.

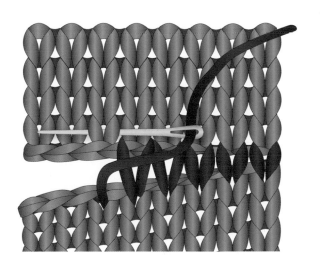

WHIPSTITCH

Thread a tapestry needle with yarn. With either the right or the wrong side of the fabric facing you, insert the tapestry needle through the center of the edge stitches, working from right to left. Start again with the next right-edge stitch, continuing upward until both edges are joined together. Make sure that the stitches are even and do not have gaps when whipping together.

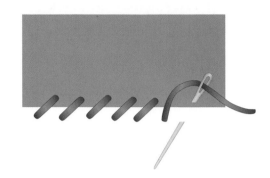

CHAIN STITCH

Insert the tapestry needle through the fabric from back to front. *Form a loop; hold the loop with your thumb. Insert the needle through the original hole from the front of the fabric to the back and bring the needle forward the desired distance. Make sure the needle is inside the loop as you pull the thread through to the front to form the chain. Repeat from *.

LAZY DAISY

Work as for the chain stitch, but anchor the loop at the top of the stitch to form petals.

SEWING

A few projects require a lining to protect the work from stains or sharp objects as well as to provide a professional finish. When selecting a lining, consider the toughness of the fabric for bags and the color choice for cases or garments. Linings can be sewn by hand (using a straight stitch) or on a sewing machine. The Finishing and Assembly instructions for each project include specific details for cutting and sewing the lining. Here are some general terms that you should be familiar with before attempting to add a lining to your project.

SEAM ALLOWANCE

The seam allowance is an extra amount of fabric added to the actual dimensions of the pattern. It creates a border, allowing you to sew the pieces together more easily.

STAY STITCHING

Stay stitching is an extra line of stitches that reinforces a seam to prevent stretching and fraying. It is typically done by machine.

ADDING AND ATTACHING A LINING

When adding a lining, first measure the dimensions of the knitted pieces, then add a ¼" (6mm) seam allowance to every side of each knitted piece, unless the pattern directions instruct otherwise. Cut and stitch around the sides of the lining. Whipstitch it to the inside of the bag or the wrong side of the project.

Secure the thread with a knot. Start at the back of the fabric, insert the sewing needle by catching two layers of fabric; then pull the thread through to the front. Insert the needle from the front to back diagonally and pull the thread through, making sure the stitches lie flat.

INSERTING A ZIPPER

1. Choose a zipper at least 2" (5.1cm) larger than the opening of the project. Place the zipper inside the project with the right side facing out. With a sharp sewing needle and matching thread, whipstitch the zipper to the inside of the project (see step 1).

2. On the front (outside) of the work, backstitch just below the zipper's teeth. Place the lining over the zipper's edge and whipstitch it into place (see step 2).

Step 1

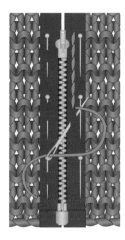

Step 2

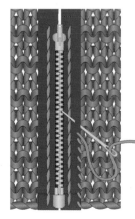

ONE BALL GIFTS

COFFEE-FOR-FOUR
TABLE COASTERS

Looking for the right coaster to slide under your mug? Dress up your coffee table with these lacy coasters, each with its own unique design. The coasters share a moss stitch border but feature four different lace designs, adding interest to your knitting as well as your home décor.

SKILL LEVEL

Steps-and-Ladder
Coaster: Easy
Wrap Coaster: Intermediate
Fan Coaster: Intermediate
Eyelet Coaster: Easy

FINISHED MEASUREMENTS

Steps-and-Ladder Coaster:
Height: 5"/12.7cm
Width: 4½"/11.4cm
Wrap Coaster, Fan Coaster,
and Eyelet Coaster:
Height: 4½"/11.4cm
Width: 5"/12.7cm

YARN

1 skein of Kollage Cornstastic
(100% corn, 50g = 105 yd/96m
per skein) in color #6506 Jade
OR approximately 105 yd/96m
lightweight corn yarn in
light green

MATERIALS

• Size 6 U.S. (4mm) needles,
  or size needed to obtain
  gauge
• Straight pins
• Stitch marker
• Tapestry needle

GAUGE

22 sts = 4"/10cm over St st
Always take time to check
your gauge.

PATTERN NOTES

• Both charts and written
  instructions for all four
  coasters are provided.
  Choose the instruction
  method you prefer.
• While the coasters may
  knit to slightly different
  measurements, you
  can block them to a
  uniform size.

SPECIAL ABBREVIATIONS

P4tog: Purl 4 sts together.
Inc 2: Increase by knitting,
purling, then knitting again
into next st, before slipping it
off needle.
Sl1wyib: Slip 1 st with yarn in
back.
Sl1wyif: Slip 1 st with yarn in
front.
Sl2wyib: Slip 2 sts with yarn in
back.
Sl2wyif: Slip 2 sts with yarn in
front.
Yo2: Yarn over 2 times.
Wrap2: (Sl2wyif, bring yarn in
back of work, slip 2 sts back to
LH needle, bring yarn to front
of work) 2 times, sl2wyif.
Ptbl: Purl 1 st through
back loop.

COASTERS

Steps-and-Ladder Coaster

CO 26 sts.
Row 1 (RS): *K1, p1; rep from
* across.
Row 2 (WS): *P1, k1; rep from
* across.
Rep Rows 1–2.
Row 5: (K1, p1) 2 times, purl
across to last 4 sts, (k1, p1)
2 times.
Row 6: (P1, k1) 2 times, knit
across to last 4 sts, (p1, k1)
2 times.
Row 7: (K1, p1) 2 times,
*sl1wyib, k1; rep from * to last
4 sts, (k1, p1) 2 times.
Row 8: (P1, k1) 2 times, *p1,
sl1wyif; rep from * to last 4 sts,
(p1, k1) 2 times.
Row 9: (K1, p1) 2 times, k1, *yo,
skp; rep from * to last 5 sts, k2,
p1, k1, p1.
Row 10: (P1, k1) 2 times, purl
across to last 3 sts, k1, p1, k1.
Row 11: K1, p1, k1, p7, (k1, p1)
3 times, k1, p5, (k1, p1) 2 times.
Row 12: P1, k1, p1, k7, (p1, k1)
3 times, p1, k5, (p1, k1) 2 times.
Row 13: (K1, p1) 2 times,
(sl1wyib, k1) 2 times, sl1wyib,
(p1, k1) 4 times, (k1, sl1wyib)
2 times, k2, p1, k1, p1.
Row 14: (P1, k1) 2 times, (p1,
sl1wyif) 2 times, p1, (k1, p1)
4 times, (sl1wyib, k1) 2 times,
sl1wyib, (p1, k1) 2 times.
Row 15: (K1, p1) 2 times, k1,
(yo, k2tog) 2 times, (p1, k1)
4 times, (yo, k2tog) 2 times,
k2, p1, k1, p1.
Row 16: (P1, k1) 2 times, p5,
(k1, p1) 3 times, k1, p7, k1, p1, k1.
Rows 17–22: Rep Rows 11–16.
Rows 23 and 24: Rep Rows 11
and 12.
Rows 25–28: Rep Rows 7–10.
Rows 29 and 30: Rep Rows 5
and 6.
Rows 31–34: Rep Rows 1–4.
BO all stitches.

Wrap Coaster

CO 28 sts.
Row 1 (RS): *K1, p1; rep from
* across.

Row 2 (WS): *P1, k1; rep from
* across.
Rep Rows 1–2.
Row 5: (K1, p1) 2 times, k2tog,
[yo2, (k2tog) 2 times] 4 times,
yo2, k2tog, (k1, p1) 2 times.
Row 6: (P1, k1) 2 times, p2,
p1tbl, *wrap2, p1, p1tbl; rep
from * 3 times, p2, k1, p1, k1.
Row 7: (K1, p1) 2 times, yo,
[(k2tog) 2 times, yo2] 4 times,
(k2tog) 2 times, yo, (k1, p1) 2
times.
Row 8: (P1, k1) 2 times, p1,
*wrap2, p1, p1tbl; rep from *
3 times, wrap2, p2, k1, p1, k1.
Row 9: (K1, p1) 2 times, k2tog,
yo2, (k2tog) 2 times, yo,
(k1, p1) 4 times, yo, (k2tog)
2 times, yo2, k2tog, (k1, p1)
2 times.
Row 10: (P1, k1) 2 times, p2,
p1tbl, wrap2, (k1, p1) 5 times,
wrap2, p1, p1tbl, p2, k1, p1, k1.
Row 11: (K1, p1) 2 times, yo,
(k2tog) 2 times, yo2, k2tog,
(k1, p1) 4 times, k2tog, yo2,
(k2tog) 2 times, yo, (k1, p1)
2 times.
Row 12: (P1, k1) 2 times, p1,
wrap2, p1, p1tbl, (k1, p1)
5 times, k1, p1tbl, wrap2, p2,
k1, p1, k1.
Rows 13–24: Rep Rows 9–12
3 times.
Row 25: Rep Row 9.
Rows 26–28: Rep Rows 6–8.
Row 29: Rep Row 5.
Row 30: Rep Row 2.
Row 31–32: Rep Rows 1–2.
Row 33: Rep Row 1.
BO all sts.

Fan Coaster
CO 24 sts.
Row 1 (RS): *K1, p1; rep from
* across.
Row 2 (WS): *P1, k1; rep from
* across.
Rep Rows 1–2.
Row 5: (K1, p1) 2 times,
(p4tog, yo) 4 times,
(k1, p1) 2 times.
Row 6: (P1, k1) 2 times, (inc 2,
k1) 4 times, (p1, k1) 2 times.
Row 7: (K1, p1) 2 times, knit
across to last 4 sts, (k1, p1)
2 times.
Row 8: (P1, k1) 2 times, (p4tog,
yo) 4 times, (p1, k1) 2 times.
Row 9: (K1, p1) 2 times, (inc 2,
k1) 4 times, (k1, p1) 2 times.
Row 10: (P1, k1) 2 times, knit
across to last 4 sts, (p1, k1)
2 times.
Row 11: (K1, p1) 2 times, p4tog,
yo, (k1, p1) 4 times, p4tog, yo,
(k1, p1) 2 times.
Row 12: (P1, k1) 2 times, inc 2,
k1, (p1, k1) 4 times, inc 2, k1,
(p1, k1) 2 times.
Row 13: (K1, p1) 2 times, knit
across to last 3 sts, p1, k1, p1.
Row 14: (P1, k1) 2 times, p4tog,
yo, (p1, k1) 4 times, p4tog, yo,
(p1, k1) 2 times.
Row 15: (K1, p1) 2 times, inc 2,
k2, (p1, k1) 3 times, p1, inc 2,
k2, p1, k1, p1.
Row 16: Rep Row 10.
Rows 17–21: Rep Rows 11–15.
Row 22: Rep Row 10.
Rows 23–27: Rep Rows 5–9.
Row 28: Rep Row 2.
Rows 29–30: Rep Rows 1–2.
Row 31: Rep Row 1.
BO all sts.

Eyelet Coaster
CO 26 sts.
Row 1 (RS): *K1, p1; rep from
* across.
Row 2 (WS): *P1, k1; rep from
* across.
Rep Rows 1–2.
Row 5: (K1, p1) 2 times, k1, *yo,
skp; rep from * to last 5 sts, k2,
p1, k1, p1.
Row 6: (P1, k1) 2 times, p1, *yo,
skp; rep from * to last 5 sts, p2,
k1, p1, k1.
Rep Rows 5–6 once more.
Row 9: (K1, p1) 2 times, k1,
(yo, skp) 2 times, k2,(p1, k1)
3 times, (yo, skp) 2 times, k2,
p1, k1, p1.
Row 10: (P1, k1) 2 times, p2,
(yo, k2tog) 2 times, p2, (k1, p1)
3 times, (yo, k2tog) 2 times,
p2, k1, p1, k1.
Rep Rows 9–10 7 times and
Row 9 once more.
Rows 26–28: Rep Rows 6–8.
Row 29: Rep Row 5.
Rows 30–32: Rep Rows 2–4.
Row 33: Rep Row 1.
BO all sts.

FINISHING AND ASSEMBLY
1. Weave in ends.
2. Block coasters.

DESIGN TIP
With one skein of this yarn,
you can knit a set of five
coasters.

STITCH

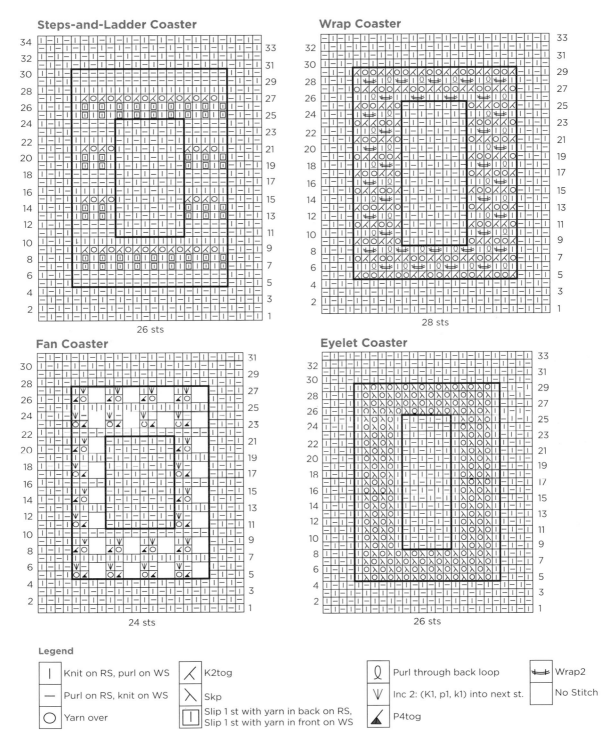

Steps-and-Ladder Coaster
26 sts

Wrap Coaster
28 sts

Fan Coaster
24 sts

Eyelet Coaster
26 sts

Legend

I	Knit on RS, purl on WS	⟋	K2tog
—	Purl on RS, knit on WS	⟍	Skp
○	Yarn over	⊡	Slip 1 st with yarn in back on RS, Slip 1 st with yarn in front on WS

Ɋ	Purl through back loop	↤↦	Wrap2
V	Inc 2: (K1, p1, k1) into next st.	▢	No Stitch
◣	P4tog		

IRISH HUE RUNNER

This table runner is a delight for the advanced beginner who's willing to give lace a try. The pattern stitch is easy, and the variegated yarn creates lacy stripes. Knit in cotton blend yarn, this project is a perfect gift. Just one ball is all you'll need to bring a bit of Ireland into someone's home.

SKILL LEVEL
Intermediate

FINISHED MEASUREMENTS
Width: 10"/25.4cm
Length: 25½"/64.8cm

YARN
1 skein of Noro Chirimen (60% cotton/24% silk/16% wool, 50g = 137 yd/125m per skein) in color #3 Kiwi-Yellow-Tan OR approximately 137 yd/125m lightweight cotton/silk/wool blend yarn in multi yellow-green-light brown

MATERIALS
• Size 7 U.S. (4.5mm) needles, or size needed to obtain gauge
• Straight pins
• Stitch marker
• Tapestry needle

GAUGE
38 sts = 10"/25.4cm over Irish Hue Lace Stitch patt. Always take time to check your gauge.

PATTERN NOTE
Both chart and written instructions for Irish Hue Lace Stitch are provided. Choose the instruction method you prefer.

SPECIAL ABBREVIATIONS
K3tog: Knit 3 sts together.
Sk2p: Slip 1 st, knit next 2 sts together. Pass the slipped st over the k2tog st and off the needle.

STITCH PATTERN
Irish Hue Lace Stitch (over 38 sts)
Row 1 (RS): K4, p2, (yo, k2tog, k1, yo, k2tog, k2) 2 times, skp, yo, k1, skp, yo, k2, skp, yo, k1, skp, yo, p2, k4.
Row 2 and all WS rows: K2, p2, k2, p26, k2, p2, k2.
Row 3: K4, p2, (yo, k2tog) 2 times, (k2, yo, k2tog) 2 times, k2, (yo, skp) 2 times, k2, yo, skp, k2, yo, skp, p2, k4.
Row 5: K4, p2, k1, (yo, k2tog, k2) 2 times, yo, k3tog, yo, k2, yo, sk2p, yo, (k2, skp, yo) 2 times, k1, p2, k4.
Row 7: K4, p2, (yo, k2tog, k2) 2 times, yo, (k2tog) 2 times, yo, k2, yo, (skp) 2 times, yo, (k2, skp, yo) 2 times, p2, k4.
Row 9: K4, p2, (yo, skp, k2) 2 times, yo, (skp) 2 times, yo, k2, yo, (k2tog) 2 times, yo, (k2, k2tog, yo) 2 times, p2, k4.
Row 11: K4, p2, k1, (yo, skp, k2) 2 times, yo, sk2p, yo, k2, yo, k3tog, yo, (k2, k2tog, yo) 2 times, k1, p2, k4.
Row 13: K4, p2, (yo, skp) 2 times, k2, yo, skp, k2, skp, yo, k2, yo, k2tog, k2, k2tog, yo, k2, (k2tog, yo) 2 times, p2, k4.
Row 15: K4, p2, yo, skp, k1, yo, skp, k2, yo, skp, k1, skp, yo, k2, yo, k2tog, k1, k2tog, yo, k2, k2tog, yo, k1, k2tog, yo, p2, k4.
Row 16: Rep Row 2.
Rep Rows 1–16 for Irish Hue Lace Stitch patt.

TABLE RUNNER
CO 38 sts. Knit 2 rows. Work Irish Hue Lace Stitch patt until table runner measures 25"/63.5cm, ending with a WS row. Knit 2 rows. BO.

FINISHING AND ASSEMBLY
1. Weave in ends.
2. Block table runner.

DESIGN TIP
Fringe may be added to the table runner. Be sure to set aside a few yards of yarn before starting the project.

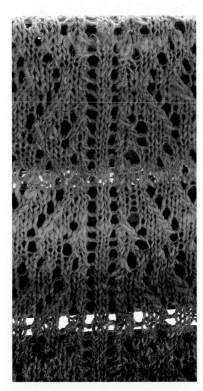

STITCH CHART
Irish Hue Lace Stitch
(over 38 sts)

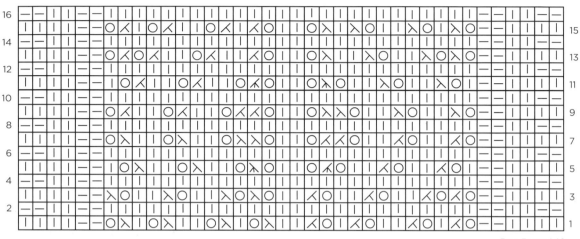

Rep Rows 1–16

Legend

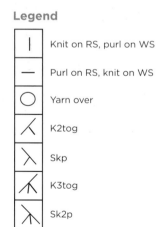

	Knit on RS, purl on WS
—	Purl on RS, knit on WS
◯	Yarn over
⟋	K2tog
⟍	Skp
⟋⟍	K3tog
⟍⟋	Sk2p

COMFY HOT-WATER BOTTLE COZY

Nobody likes feeling under the weather, but this lovely hot-water bottle cozy, knit in the round and featuring delicate cables, is sure to soothe a friend or loved one in need of comfort.

SKILL LEVEL
Intermediate

FINISHED MEASUREMENTS
Length: 14"/35.6cm
Circumference: 15"/38.1cm

YARN
1 hank of Blue Sky Alpaca Suri Merino (60% baby suri/40% merino, 100g = 164 yd/150m) in color #411 Cloud OR approximately 164 yd/150m lightweight baby suri/merino blend yarn in light blue

MATERIALS
- Size 7 U.S. (4.5mm) double-pointed or circular needle, or size needed to obtain gauge
- Cable needle
- Stitch marker
- Tapestry needle
- Sewing thread
- 1 2-qt (2L) water bottle,
- 14 x 8"/35.6 x 20.3cm
- 6"/15cm of elastic, ¼" (0.6cm) wide
- Safety pin

GAUGE
24 sts = 4"/10cm over patt st
Always take time to check your gauge.

PATTERN NOTES
- Both chart and written instructions for Comfy Cable Stitch are provided. Choose the instruction method you prefer.
- The piece will be knitted in the round and seamed at the bottom. A casing will be formed by folding over the top edge and drawing elastic through it.
- For instructions on whipstitching, see page XX.

SPECIAL ABBREVIATIONS
4-st Right Cable: Slip 2 sts to cable needle and hold in back of work, k2, k2 from cable needle.
4-st Left Cable: Slip 2 sts to cable needle and hold in front of work, k2, k2 from cable needle.

STITCH PATTERN
Comfy Cable Stitch (over a multiple of 10 sts)
Rnds 1–7: *K2, p4, k2, p2; rep from * around.
Rnds 8–9: *K8, p2; rep from * around.
Rnd 10: *4-st Right Cable, 4-st Left Cable, p2; rep from * around.
Rnds 11–13: *K8, p2; rep from * around.
Rnd 14: *4-st Left Cable, 4-st Right Cable, p2; rep from * around.
Rnds 15–16: *K8, p2; rep from * around.
Rep Rnds 1–16 for Comfy Cable Stitch patt.

WATER BOTTLE
CO 90 sts. Pm at beg of rnd and join, being careful not to twist sts.
Work Rnds 8–16 once, then work Rnds 1–16 3 times for Comfy Cable Stitch patt.

Rib Rounds
Next Rnd: *K2, p1, k2, p1, k2, p2; rep from * around.
Rep this rnd 5 more times.

Decrease Round
Next Rnd: *K2, p1, k2, p1, k2, p2tog; rep from * around.
Next Rnd: *K2, p1; rep from * around.
Rep last rnd until piece measures 1¾"/4.5cm from beg. BO.

FINISHING AND ASSEMBLY
1. Weave in ends.
2. Sew cast-on edges together.
3. Measure elastic around the lip of the water bottle, making sure it fits snugly.
4. Cut elastic.
5. Fold top ½" (1.3cm) of knitted edge to inside (WS), forming a casing. Whipstitch into place, leaving a small slit for inserting elastic.
6. Open safety pin and poke tip through top edge of elastic. Close safety pin.

STITCH CHART
Comfy Cable Stitch
(over a multiple of 10 sts)

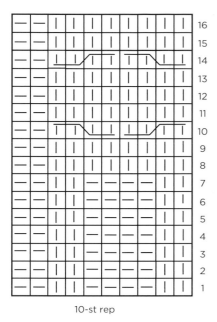

10-st rep

Rep Rounds 8–16 once,
then Rounds 1–16 3 times

Legend

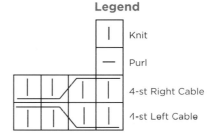

	Knit
—	Purl
	4-st Right Cable
	4-st Left Cable

7. Slip safety pin through the slit and ease around the top edge, pulling elastic around.
8. Pull safety pin through slit on other side. Tack the elastic edges together with sewing thread.
9. Whipstitch the opening.
10. Weave in any loose ends.
11. Slip cozy over the water bottle.

DESIGN TIP
Instead of using elastic around the neck of the cozy, you can add a drawstring. Leave a small opening at one edge of the casing to slip a drawstring through.

SQUARE ELEGANCE LACE BOWL

Your special someone will be delighted to receive this beautiful knitted lace bowl. The traditional beauty of the lace contrasts with the simple stockinette stitch to create a wonderful addition to any décor. Just knit and starch the lace bowl, and in a few hours you will have an impressive gift.

SKILL LEVEL
Intermediate

FINISHED MEASUREMENTS
Length: 10"/25.4cm
Width: 8½"/21.6cm
Depth: 4"/10.2cm

YARN
1 skein of Crystal Palace Panda Cotton (50% bamboo/25% cotton/16% elastic nylon, 50g = 182 yd/168m per skein) in color #0204 Ivory OR approximately 182 yd/168m lightweight bamboo/cotton/elastic/nylon yarn in ivory

MATERIALS
- Size 6 U.S. (4mm) needles, or size needed to obtain gauge
- Cable needle
- Straight pins
- Stitch marker
- Tapestry needle
- Plaid Stiffy Fabric Stiffener 8 fl oz./236 ml OR fabric stiffener/starch
- Large bowl for molding
- Iron (optional)

GAUGE
24 sts and 30 rows = 4"/10cm over St st
Always take time to check your gauge.

PATTERN NOTES
- When attaching the two pieces of the base, turn them in opposite directions so each lace section will be next to a stockinette section, as shown in the schematic.
- Once joined, the knitted pieces will be ironed, starched, and molded.
- On Row 2, extra yos are dropped off the needle to form elongated stitches, maintaining the original stitch count. The cable pattern is worked over the remaining yos.
- A large metal bowl is preferred for molding.
- For instructions on whipstitching, refer to page 36.

SPECIAL ABBREVIATIONS
K-yo3: Knit by wrapping yarn 3 times around the needle. Extra yos will be dropped on the next row to form elongated sts, maintaining the original st count.
Inc1: Increase 1 st by knitting into the front, then into the back of the same st before slipping it off the needle.
C6B: Slip 3 elongated sts to cable needle and hold to back of work, knit 3 elongated sts, knit 3 from cable needle.

STITCH PATTERN
Square Elegance Lace Stitch
(over a multiple of 6 sts + 2)
Row 1 (RS): K1, *k-yo3; rep from * across to last st, k1.
Row 2 (WS): K1, * (drop 2 yos per yo st left on LH needle) 6 times, C6B; rep from * to last st, k1.
Row 3: Knit.
Row 4: Knit.
Rep Rows 1–4 5 times and Rows 1–3 once for Square Elegance Lace Stitch patt.

LACE BOWL
Base (Make 2)
CO 32 sts. Knit 2 rows. Work Square Elegance Lace Stitch for 23 rows, ending with Row 3.
Next Row (WS): Purl across to last st, k1.
Next Row (RS): Knit.
Rep last 2 rows for 4½"/11.4cm, ending on RS. Knit next 2 rows. BO all sts.

STITCH CHART
Square Elegance Lace Stitch
(over a multiple of 6 sts + 2)

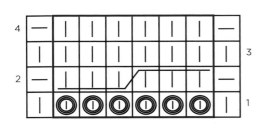

Legend

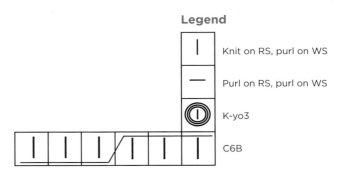

|	Knit on RS, purl on WS
—	Purl on RS, purl on WS
◎	K-yo3
	C6B

SCHEMATIC

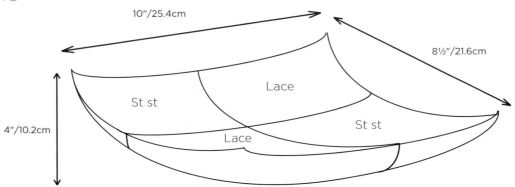

10"/25.4cm

8½"/21.6cm

4"/10.2cm

St st

Lace

Lace

St st

FINISHING AND ASSEMBLY

1. Weave in loose ends.
2. Iron wrong side of knitted pieces on lowest setting or block gently.
3. Place pieces side by side so each lace section is next to a stockinette section, as shown in the schematic. Whipstitch together.
4. Turn bowl upside down.
5. Place WS of knitted piece over the bottom of the bowl, with the RS fabric facing you. Be sure the bowl is bigger than the lace.
6. Following manufacturer's instructions, apply starch or stiffener to right side of knitted piece, with hand or brush, saturating the fabric.
7. Mold and adjust knitted base until length of each side corresponds to given finished measurements.
8. Let dry overnight.
9. Remove knitted bowl gently from mold. Keep bowl away from drafts.

DESIGN TIP
Be sure the bowl you're using to mold your starched knitted piece has a smooth exterior.

MINI SLING BACKPACK

Your favorite fashion-forward teen will love this bag—it's small in size but big on style. All-over lace stitch, felted straps, and leather drawstrings and base make this the "right" bag for the "right" girl.

SKILL LEVEL
Intermediate

FINISHED MEASUREMENTS
Height: 10"/25.4cm
Width at base: 8½"/21.6cm

YARN
1 skein of Brown Sheep Lamb's Pride (85% wool/15% mohair, 113g = 190 yd/174m per skein) in color #M62 Amethyst OR approximately 190 yd/174m worsted-weight wool/mohair yarn in purple

MATERIALS
- Size 9 U.S. (5.5mm) double-pointed or circular needle, or size needed to obtain gauge
- Straight pins
- Stitch marker
- Tapestry needle
- Embroidery scissors
- 1 package (18 pcs) BagWorks Additions 9.2mm Eyelets, #A3019-GLD in gold OR twelve 9.2mm gold eyelets
- 1 8½ x 11" (21.6 x 28cm) Tandy Leather Factory Cowhide Suede Trim Piece, #4040-04 Sand OR 8½ x 11" (21.6 x 28cm) piece of cowhide suede trim in tan
- 1 30"/76.2cm Leather Cord USA 5mm Roving Leather Cord, #01-Natural OR 1 30"/76.2cm 5mm leather cord in natural

- 1 package (4 pcs) BagWorks Additions Silver Crimp, #A3115-SIL OR two ½" (1.3cm) silver crimps
- ¼ yd (25cm) lining fabric of your choice
- Cotton thread to match lining
- Sewing needle
- Pliers (optional)
- Hammer

GAUGE
16 sts = 4"/10cm over St st
Always take time to check your gauge.

PATTERN NOTES
- The bag is knitted in the round with a hem forming a casing at the top edge. The base is cut from suede. A pair of linings is sewn to match the body and base of the bag. After attaching the base to the knitted body, the lining is attached, the eyelets are placed, and the cording is woven through the eyelets.
- The strap is knitted, lightly felted, cut in half, and attached to the back of the backpack.
- Both chart and written instructions for Right Carrier Lace Stitch are provided. Choose the instruction method you prefer.
- For instructions on felting, see page 33.
- For instructions on whipstitching, see page 36.

SPECIAL ABBREVIATIONS
Garter stitch: Knit every row.
Sk2p: Slip 1 st, k2tog, and pass the slipped st over the knit st.

STITCH PATTERN
Right Carrier Lace Stitch (over a multiple of 4 sts + 1)
Rnd 1: Yo, *k1, yo, sk2p, yo; rep from * across to last 4 sts, sk2p, yo, k1, yo.
Rnd 2: *Sk2p, yo, k1, yo; rep from * to last 3 sts, sk2p.
Rep Rnds 1 and 2 for Right Carrier Lace Stitch patt.

PURSE
Body
With circular needle, CO 89 sts. Pm at beg of rnd and join, being careful not to twist.
Preparation Round:
Purl around.
Work Rnds 1–2 of Right Carrier Lace Stitch patt until piece measures 9"/23cm from cast-on edge.

Hem
Next Rnd: Knit.
Next Rnd: *Yo, k2tog, k5, yo, k2tog, k6; rep from * to last 7 sts, yo, k2tog, k5.
Knit next 2 rnds. Purl 1 rnd.
Knit next 4 rnds. BO.

Strap
CO 4 sts. Work in garter stitch for 216 rows (108 ridges).

FELTING STRAP

Felt the knitted strap lightly. Check frequently to make sure the strap does not shrink to a length of less than 34"/86.4cm. Cut strap in 2 pieces, each 17"/43.18cm long.

FINISHING AND ASSEMBLY

1. Weave in ends of knitted pieces.
2. Cut one suede oval 8½ x 4½"/21.6 x 11.4cm in diameter for base (see schematic).
3. Cut one 30"/76cm length of leather cording for drawstring.
4. Using the body and base as guides, and subtracting ½"/1.3cm from top of body and, *at the same time,* adding ¼"/0.6cm seam allowance all around, cut 2 linings for each piece. Sew body lining to base lining. Repeat for other body and base lining. Place one lining inside the other, WS facing and RS out.
5. Punch 41 (or an odd number of) small holes ½"/1.3cm apart around leather base.
6. Thread tapestry needle with yarn and attach leather base to knitted body by whipstitching around base. When the last hole is stitched, whipstitch in the opposite direction using the same holes to create a cross-stitch edging around base.
7. Weave in remaining ends.
8. Mark lining for eyelet holes as follows: Place lining inside of bag and fold the knitted hem over lining. Lining can now be seen through the yo holes. Mark through yos on to lining with chalk or pencil.
9. With embroidery scissors, slit or poke holes in lining that can easily accommodate your eyelets.
10. Following manufacturer's directions, hammer eyelets down through knitted yos and marked holes in lining.
11. Whipstitch knitted hem over the lining.
12. Center felted straps on back of backpack. Pin in place 3"/7.6cm from top, 2"/5cm from bottom, and 5½"/14cm apart measuring from center of each strap. If recipient's shoulders are narrow, you may want to move the upper edges of straps in a bit. Whipstitch in place and secure.
13. Pull cording through eyelets. Slide silver crimps to 1"/2.5cm from edge of cording. Crimp in place with pliers.

DESIGN TIP

Be sure to use a tough lining fabric to make a sturdy bag.

STITCH CHART
Right Carrier Lace Stitch
(over a multiple of 4 sts + 1)

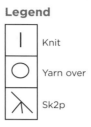

Legend

|	Knit
O	Yarn over
⋏	Sk2p

SCHEMATICS

Suede Base

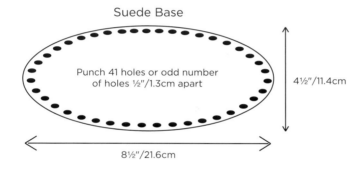

Punch 41 holes or odd number
of holes ½"/1.3cm apart

4½"/11.4cm

8½"/21.6cm

Back of Backpack

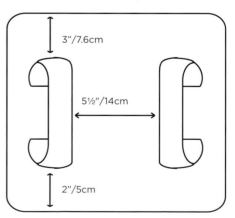

3"/7.6cm

5½"/14cm

2"/5cm

INTERLOCKING SQUARE PILLOW

Even a beginner can knit this modern-looking pillow, which makes a great housewarming gift. Four I-cords placed geometrically on a Stockinette Stitch background give a contemporary flair to any room.

SKILL LEVEL
Easy

FINISHED MEASUREMENTS
Length: 11"/28cm
Width: 11"/28cm

YARN
1 skein of Berroco Comfort DK (50% Super-Fine Nylon/50% Super Fine Acrylic, 1.75 oz/50g = 178 yd/165m per skein) in color #2760 Beet Root OR approximately 178 yd/165m DK-weight nylon/acrylic blend yarn in deep burgundy

MATERIALS
- Size 8 U.S. (5mm) needles, or size needed to obtain gauge
- Tapestry needle
- Sewing thread
- Sewing needle
- ½ yd (45.7cm) decorative fabric of your choice for pillow back
- 1 11 x 11" (28 x 28cm) pillow form OR
- ½ yd (45.7cm) muslin or lightweight cotton fabric of your choice
- 1 bag of Poly-fil (100% polyester fiberfill, 12 oz) OR one 12 oz bag of polyester fiberfill

GAUGE
22 sts = 4"/10cm over St st
Always take time to check your gauge.

PATTERN NOTES
- Place I-cord on the pillow back according to schematic.
- If purchased pillow form is not used, a fabric pillow form is sewn and placed inside the knitted pillow.
- For instructions on whipstitching, see page 36.
- For instructions on making I-cord, see page 29.

STITCH PATTERN
Stockinette Stitch (St st)
Row 1: Knit.
Row 2: Purl.
Rep Rows 1–2 for Stockinette Stitch patt.

PILLOW
Cording
For pillow, make a total of 4 I-cords as follows:
(Make 2) CO 4 sts, work I-cord until cord measures 18"/45.7cm. BO all sts.
(Make 2) CO 4 sts, work I-cord until cord measures 16"/40.6cm. BO all sts.

Pillow Front
CO 53 sts. Work in St st until piece measures 12"/30.5cm from cast-on edge. BO all sts.

Pillow Back
Using pillow front as template, cut out 1 square for the back of the pillow from the decorative fabric.

Pillow Form (if pillow form is not purchased)
Using pillow back as template, cut 2 pieces of muslin. Sew along 3 sides of the pillow form and most of the 4th side, leaving opening large enough to insert stuffing. Turn fabric inside out through the slit. Stuff pillow with fiber to desired firmness. Sew remaining seam, turning edges to inside of pillow form.

SCHEMATIC

16"/40.6cm I-Cord

18"/45.7cm I-Cord →

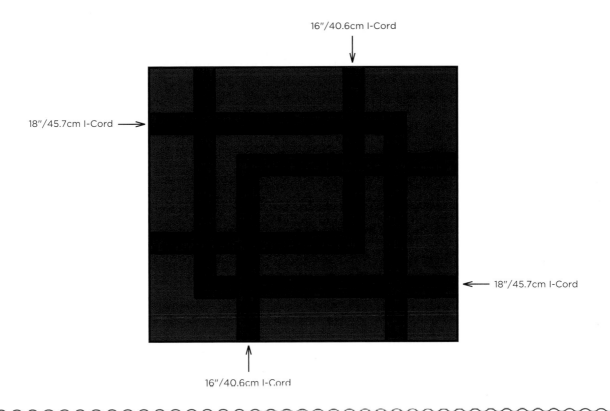

← 18"/45.7cm I-Cord

16"/40.6cm I-Cord

FINISHING AND ASSEMBLY

1. Weave in ends.
2. Block knitted front to 11 x 11"/28 x 28cm.
3. Using schematic as a guide, pin cording to pillow front.
4. Thread sewing needle. Attach I-cord to pillow front by stitching from beneath the pillow front up through the I-cord.
5. Attach pillow back to knitted pillow front by whipstitching right sides together. Leave one side unstitched. Turn RS out.
6. Place pillow form inside knitted cover.
7. Whipstitch the opening.

DESIGN TIP

For a dramatic look, twist the I-cord with colored or metallic cording before attaching it to the pillow.

BERRY PRETTY KNITTING BASKET

Yarn, needles, knitting projects in progress, and just about anything else will fit perfectly in this basket. Our Berry Loop Stitch with cables adorns this easy-to-knit cover that turns a functional craft basket into a decorative accessory.

SKILL LEVEL
Easy

FINISHED MEASUREMENTS
Small Side Panel
Height: 6"/15.2cm
Base Width: 8½"/21.6cm

Large Side Panel
Height: 6"/15.2cm
Base Width: 12"/30.5cm

Base
Length: 8½"/21.6cm
Width: 12"/30.5cm

Basket
14 x 8½ x 6"/35.5 x 21.6 x 15.2cm

YARN
1 skein of Bernat Satin Sport Solid (100% acrylic, 3 oz/85g = 221 yd/202m per skein) in color #03430 Wine OR approximately 221 yd/202m lightweight acrylic yarn in deep burgundy

MATERIALS
- Size 6 U.S. (4mm) needles, or size needed to obtain gauge
- Straight pins
- Stitch marker
- Tapestry needle
- Sewing thread to match yarn color
- 1 14 x 8½ x 6"/35.5 x 21.6 x 15.2cm lined basket

GAUGE
22 sts and 26 rows = 4"/10cm over St st
Always take time to check your gauge.

PATTERN NOTES
- Both chart and written instructions for Berry Loop Stitch are provided. Choose the instruction method you prefer.
- The panels will be stretched to fit the basket.
- To assemble, first join together the 4 side panels and place them over the basket. Then place the base over the bottom of the basket, stretch it, and stitch it to the bottom of the side panels.
- For instructions on whipstiching, see page 36.

SPECIAL ABBREVIATIONS
Inc 1: Knit into front, then into back of st.
Sk2p: Slip 1 st, knit next 2 sts together. Pass the slipped st over the k2tog st and off the needle.
P-inc 1: Purl into front, then into back of st.
Loop: Insert RH needle from the front into center of sk2p st of the previous row. Wrap yarn around RH needle and draw it forward, forming a loop. Leave loop on RH needle.
Loop2Cable: Make 1 loop (see Loop), slip loop to cable needle and hold in front of work. P2, slip loop onto RH needle.
Smocking Loop St: With yarn in back, insert RH needle between the 6th and 7th sts on the LH needle. Wrap yarn around RH needle and draw it forward, forming a loop. Slip this loop onto the LH needle and knit it together with the first st on the LH needle.

STITCH PATTERN
Berry Loop Stitch
Row 1 (RS): K3, *p3, sk2p; rep from * to last 6 sts, p3, k3.
Row 2: Knit the knit sts, purl the purl sts, and sk2p sts.
Row 3: K3, p2, *loop, p1, loop2cable, p1; rep from * to last 4 sts, p1, k3.
Row 4: *P3, k3; rep from * across.
Row 5: Knit the k sts, purl the p sts.
Row 6: Inc 1, *knit the k sts, purl the p sts; rep from * across to last st, inc 1.
Row 7: K1, *knit the k sts, purl the p sts; rep from * across to last st, k1.
Rows 8–10: Knit the k sts, purl the p sts.
Row 11: K1, *(p3, sk2p); rep from * across to last 7 sts, sk2p, p3, k1.
Row 12: P-inc 1, *(k3, p1); rep from * to last 4 sts, p3, p-inc 1.
Row 13: K2, p2, *loop, p1, loop2cable, p1, rep from * to last 3 sts, p3.

Row 14: K2, *(p3, k3); rep from * to last 5 sts, p3, k2.

Rows 15–17: Knit the k sts, purl the p sts.

Row 18: Inc 1, * knit the k sts, purl the p sts; rep from * across to last st, inc 1.

Rows 19–20: Knit the k sts, purl the p sts.

Row 21: *(P3, sk2p); rep from * to last 3 sts, p3.

Rows 1–21 form Berry Loop Stitch patt.

BASKET

Small Side Panel (Make 2)

CO 45 sts.

Row 1 (RS): *(P3, k3); rep from * to last 3 sts, p3.

Row 2 and all WS rows: Purl the p sts, knit the k sts. *At the same time*, inc first and last st every 6th row throughout entire panel. Work until panel measures 4"/10cm from cast-on edge, ending on RS (53 sts on needle).

Next Row (WS): Cont in patt, work 19 sts, bind off 15 sts, work 19 sts.

Right Section of Small Panel

Work in patt for 1½"/3.8cm more, cont increases at right edge as established (20 sts). BO all sts.

Left Section of Small Panel

Reattach yarn on right edge of left section. Work as for right section, continuing increases at left edge as established (20 sts). BO all sts.

Large Side Panel (Make 2)

CO 63 sts

Row 1 (RS): *(P3, k3) across to last 3 sts, p3.

Row 2 and all WS rows: Purl the p sts, knit the k sts. *At the same time*, increase first and last st every 6th row 3 times, ending on WS (69 sts). Work Rows 1–21 of Berry Loop Stitch patt. BO all sts.

Base

CO 33 sts.

Row 1 (RS): *K3, p3; rep from * to last 3 sts, k3.

Row 2 (WS): Knit the k sts, purl the p sts.

Rep Rows 1–2 until piece measures 12"/30.5cm.

FINISHING AND ASSEMBLY

1. Weave in ends.
2. Block knitted pieces to measurements shown in schematic. This may require stretching and pulling.
3. Whipstitch sides of knitted side panels, leaving base open. Place connected panels around basket.
4. Turn basket upside down. Attach knitted base to bottom of basket.
5. Thread sewing needle with cotton sewing thread and whipstitch top edges of knitted panels to inner lining of basket.

DESIGN TIP

The knitted pieces are purposely made a bit smaller than the basket to give a snug fit after blocking.

STITCH CHART
Berry Loop Stitch Pattern
(over a multiple of 6 sts plus 3)

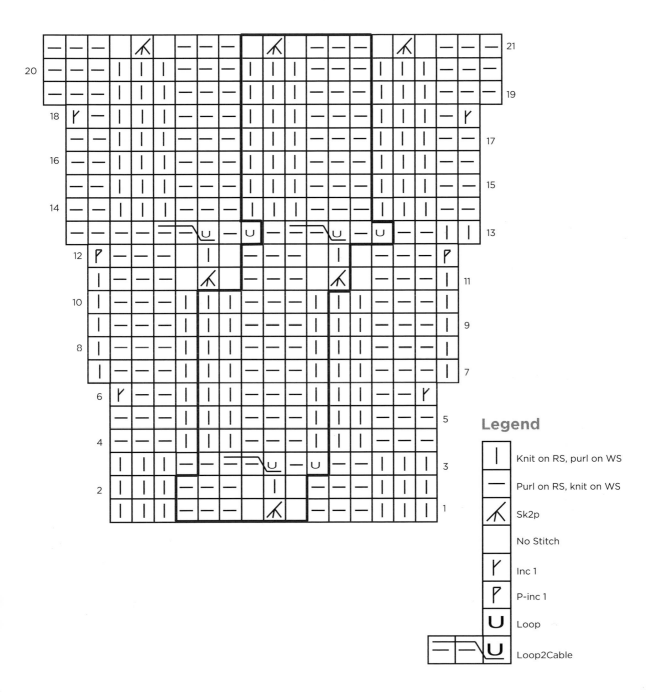

Legend

│	Knit on RS, purl on WS
—	Purl on RS, knit on WS
⋏	Sk2p
	No Stitch
Y	Inc 1
P	P-inc 1
U	Loop
U	Loop2Cable

SCHEMATICS

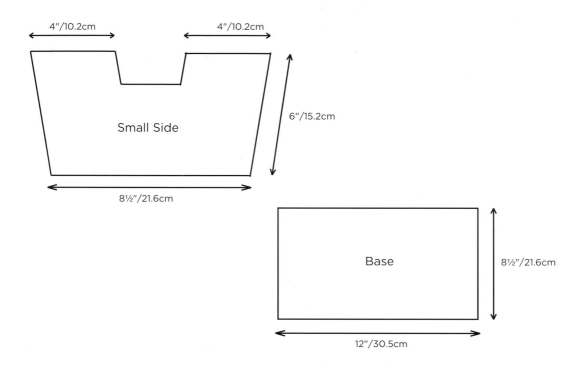

4"/10.2cm   4"/10.2cm

Small Side

6"/15.2cm

8½"/21.6cm

Base

8½"/21.6cm

12"/30.5cm

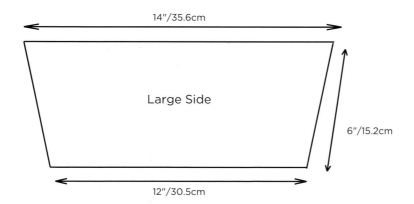

14"/35.6cm

Large Side

6"/15.2cm

12"/30.5cm

FLUFFY DENIM BOMBER HAT

Finally, a super-warm knitted hat that kids will actually want to wear.
A simple cable rings the base of the lightly felted crown, attaching it
to the earflaps, which can be worn down or secured over the crown.
Spruced up with a fur lining, this project makes a wonderfully warm
one-ball gift.

SKILL LEVEL
Easy

FINISHED MEASUREMENTS
Circumference: 22"/56cm
Fits children 4 to 6 years old.

YARN
1 skein of Patons Classic Wool (100% pure new wool, 3.5 oz/100g = 223 yd/205m per skein) in color #77115 New Denim OR approximately 223 yd/205m medium-weight wool yarn in denim

MATERIALS
- Size 9 U.S. (5.5mm) double-pointed and circular needles, or size to obtain gauge
- Stitch marker
- Tapestry needle
- Cable needle
- Sewing needle and cotton thread
- Measuring tape
- Scissors
- Hammer
- ½ yd (46.7cm) Clifton Associates' Shag fake fur in #16 Gray OR ½ yd (46.7cm) of shag fake fur in gray
- 1 Dritz Heavy Duty Snap Kit (7 snap sets and tools), Size 24 (⅝"/1.6cm) OR one ⅝"/1.6cm snap set in size 24

GAUGE
16 sts = 4"/10cm over St st
Always take time to check your gauge.

PATTERN NOTES
- Both chart and written instructions are provided for Fluffy Denim Cable Stitch. Choose the instruction method you prefer.
- The crown of the hat is knitted in the round. Begin with circular needle, then switch to double-pointed needles as indicated.
- The crown, earflaps, crown flap, and tabs are felted to measurements shown in schematics.
- Snaps are added at the bottom of the tabs according to manufacturer's instructions.
- For instructions on felting, refer to page 33.
- For instructions on whipstiching, refer to page 36.

SPECIAL ABBREVIATIONS
4-st Right Purl Twist: Slip 3 sts to cable needle and hold in back of work, k1, (p1, k1, p1) from cable needle.

4-st Left Knit Twist: Slip 1 st to cable needle and hold in front of work, (k1, p1, k1), k1 from cable needle.

4-st Left Purl Twist: Slip 1 st to cable needle and hold in front of work, (p2, k1), k1 from cable needle.

4-st Right Knit Twist: Slip 3 sts to cable needle and hold in back of work, k1, (k1, p2) from cable needle.

K3tog: Knit 3 sts together.
P3tog: Purl 3 sts together.
Sk2p: Slip 1 st, knit next 2 sts together. Pass the slipped stitch over the 2 sts knit together.
Sp2p: Slip 1 st, purl next 2 sts together. Pass the slipped st over the 2 sts purled together.

STITCH PATTERNS
Garter-Rib Stitch
Row 1 (RS): Knit.
Row 2 (WS): Knit.
Row 3: Knit.
Row 4: Purl.
Rep Rows 1–4 for Garter Rib Stitch patt.

Fluffy Denim Cable Stitch (over 12 sts)
Row 1 (RS): K1, p3, k4, p4.
Row 2 (WS): K4, p4, k4.
Row 3: K1, p1, 4-st Right Purl Twist, 4-st Left Knit Twist, p2.
Row 4: K2, (p1, k1) 3 times, p3, k1.
Row 5: (K1, p1) 4 times, k2, p2.
Rep Rows 4 and 5 2 times more. Rep Row 4 once.
Row 11: K1, p1, 4-st Left Purl Twist, 4-st Right Knit Twist, p2.
Rows 12, 14, and 16: Rep Row 2.
Rows 13, 15, and 17: Rep Row 1.
Row 18: Rep Row 2.
Rep Rows 1–18 for Fluffy Denim Cable Stitch patt.

BOMBER HAT
Crown
With circular needle, CO 90 sts, pm at beg of rnd, and join, being careful not to twist sts.

Knit 1 rnd. Purl 1 rnd.
*Knit 2 rnds, Purl 1 rnd; rep from * 7 times more.
Next Rnd: *P2tog, p8; rep from * around (81 sts).
Next Rnd: Knit.
Next Rnd: *K2tog, k7; rep from * around (72 sts).
Next Rnd: Purl.
Next Rnd: *K2tog, k6; rep from * around (63 sts).
Switch to dpns.
Next Rnd: Knit.
Next Rnd: *P2tog, p5; rep from * around (54 sts).
Next Rnd: Knit.
Next Rnd: *K2tog, k4; rep from * around (45 sts).
Next Rnd: Purl.
Next Rnd: *K2tog, k3; rep from * around (36 sts).
Next Rnd: Knit.
Next Rnd: *P2tog, p2; rep from * around (27 sts).
Next Rnd: Knit.
Next Rnd: *K2tog, k1 rep from * around (18 sts).
Next Rnd: Purl.
Next Rnd: (K2tog) 9 times (9 sts).
Next Rnd: Knit.
Next Rnd: (P2tog) 4 times, p1 (5 sts).
Cut yarn. Using tapestry needle, pull yarn through remaining sts to secure. Set aside Crown for felting.

Crown Flap

CO 30 sts. Beg Garter Rib Stitch patt. Work Rows 1–4 4 times and Row 1 once.
Row 18 (WS): Sk2p, knit across to last 3 sts, k3tog (26 sts).
Row 19: Sk2p, knit across to last 3 sts, k3tog (22 sts).
Row 20: Sp2p, purl across to last 3 sts, p3tog (18 sts).
Row 21: Sk2p, knit across to last 3 sts, k3tog (14 sts).
Rep Rows 18–20 one more time.
Next Row: Skp.
Cut yarn. Pull yarn through remaining st to secure. Set aside Crown Flap for felting.

Earflaps (Make 2)

CO 22 sts. Beg Garter Rib Stitch patt. Work Rows 1–4 4 times and Row 1 once.
Row 18 (WS): Sk2p, knit across to last 3 sts, k3tog.
Row 19: Knit across.
Row 20: Sp2p, purl across to last 3 sts, p3tog.
Row 21: Knit across.
Rep Rows 18–21 until 6 sts remain on needle.
Next Row: Sk2p, k3tog.
Next Row: Skp.
Cut yarn. Pull yarn through remaining st to secure. Set aside Earflaps for felting.

Tab Fastener (Make 2)

CO 9 sts.
Work in garter stitch (knit every row) for 3¼"/8.3cm.
BO all sts. Set aside Tab Fasteners for felting.

Cable Panel

CO 12 sts. Work Fluffy Denim Cable Stitch patt until panel measures 12"/30.5cm. BO all sts. Set aside. Do not felt.

FELTING

Note: Felt Crown, Crown Flap, Earflaps, and Tab Fasteners only. Do not felt Cable Panel. It generally takes 10 to 15 minutes to machine-felt the fabric. Check fabric frequently during felting and stop the process when fabric has shrunk to desired size. The outer edge will be looser than the rest of the fabric. The felted fabric should be larger than the dimensions given in the construction diagram.

FINISHING AND ASSEMBLY

1. Cut and shape the felted pieces according to the construction diagram.
2. Weave in ends on Cable Panel. Block Cable Panel.
3. Thread tapestry needle with yarn and whipstitch Cable Panel to cast-on edge of Crown, leaving a 6"/15.2cm space in front of hat.
4. Measure inside of Crown including Cable Panel, Crown Flap, and Earflaps. Cut fur, adding ¼"/0.6cm extra seam allowance on all sides.
5. Whipstitch felted Earflaps to front sides of Crown, under Cable Panel edges. Use construction diagram as a guide.

6. Thread sewing needle with cotton thread and using construction diagram as a guide, whipstitch fur crown and fur earflaps together. Leave a 6"/15.2cm space between earflaps in front of hat.

7. Thread sewing needle with cotton thread and whipstitch fur interior inside of Crown, turning in ¼"/0.6cm hem around edge. Leave a 2"/5cm gap on bottom edge of each Earflap for tab placement.

8. Insert ¼"/0.6cm of tab edge between gap of felt and fur of earflap. Rep for other side. Whipstitch to secure.

9. Thread sewing needle with cotton thread; attach crown flap fur to felted Crown Flap.

10. With fur side facing outward, whipstitch crown flap along 6"/15.2cm gap at front of Crown.

11. Attach heavy-duty snaps to the middle of tabs, following manufacturer's instructions. Right tab–RS (place cap), WS (place socket, bowl side up). Left tab–WS (place post), RS (place stud, raised side up).

12. Fold bottom edge of left tab 1"/2.5cm over post. Whipstitch over post to hide. Weave in any loose ends.

DESIGN TIP
This hat is perfect for either a boy or a girl.

STITCH CHART
Fluffy Denim Cable Stitch

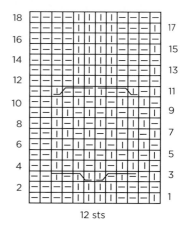

12 sts

Legend

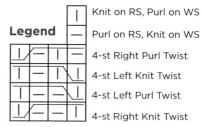

	Knit on RS, Purl on WS
—	Purl on RS, Knit on WS
	4-st Right Purl Twist
	4-st Left Knit Twist
	4-st Left Purl Twist
	4-st Right Knit Twist

SCHEMATIC/CONTRUCTION/
CUTTING DIAGRAM

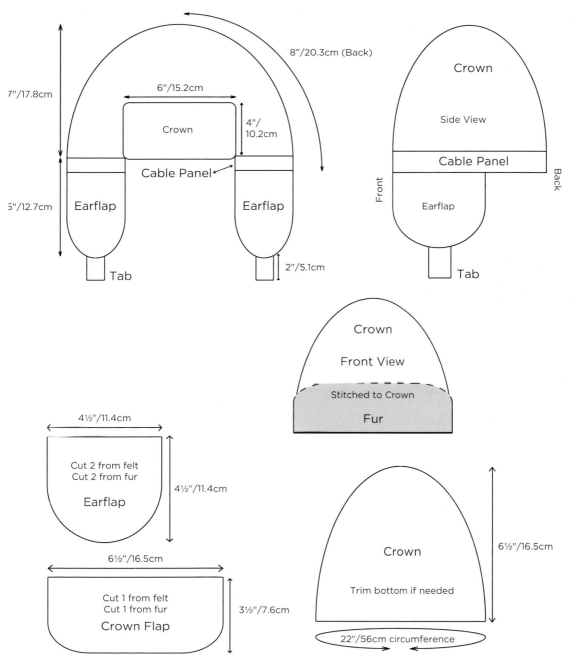

CUTE 'N' COZY TEA COZY

Tea cozies are cute and practical; and this one, with its cutwork and embellishments, will display your knitting skills at their best. Adorned with bobbles and an embellished felted body and decorated with a bell edging, this portable project is perfect for an intermediate knitter. You can have this cozy ready to give by teatime. Who says that one ball can't work wonders?

SKILL LEVEL
Intermediate

FINISHED MEASUREMENTS
Height: 8"/20.3cm
Diameter of base:
10½"/26.7cm

YARN
1 skein of Brown Sheep Nature Spun (100% wool, 3.5 oz/100g = 245 yd/224m per skein) in color #N78 Turquoise Wonder OR approximately 245 yd/224m medium-weight wool yarn in turquoise

MATERIALS
- Size 8 U.S. (5mm) needles, or size needed to obtain gauge
- Cable needle
- Straight pins
- Stitch marker
- Tapestry needle
- Embroidery needle, size 22
- 1 skein DMC pearl cotton size 5 (100% cotton, 27.3 yd/25m) in #725 OR approximately 27.3 yd/25m size 5 cotton embroidery thread in topaz yellow
- Teapot size 9 x 6 x 7¼"/22.9 x 15.3 x 18.4cm, 6-cup capacity
- Gauge

16 sts = 4"/10cm over St st
Always take time to check your gauge.

PATTERN NOTES
- Both charts and written instructions are provided for Tea Top Bobble Stitch (Chart A), Right Section Bobble Stitch (Chart B), and Left Section Bobble Stitch (Chart C). Choose the instruction method you prefer.
- The top, handle, and spout are knitted separately. The side panel is felted and cut.
- "Tea" is embroidered in chain stitch on one side of the side panel. A heart shape is cut out on the other side of the panel.
- To prevent the cut-out heart from losing shape, stabilize the cut-out edge with stay stitch.
- The top, handle, and spout are whipstitched to the panel.
- Stitches are picked up from the bottom of the tea cozy and knitted into a ruffled edging.
- For instructions on felting, refer to page 33.
- For instructions on whipstiching, refer to page 36.
- For instructions on chain stitch, refer to page 36.
- For instructions on stay stitch, refer to page 37.

SPECIAL ABBREVIATIONS
RT: Slip 1 st to cable needle, hold in back of work, k1, k1 from cable needle.

LT: Slip 1 st to cable needle, hold in front of work, k1, k1 from cable needle.
2-st Right Purl Twist: Slip 1 st to cable needle, hold in back of work, k1, p1 from cable needle.
2-st Left Purl Twist: Slip 1 st to cable needle, hold in front of work, p1, k1 from cable needle.
C3B: Slip 2 sts to cable needle, hold in back of work, k1, p2 from cable needle.
C3F: Slip 1 st to cable needle, hold in front of work, p2, k1 from cable needle.
K3tog: Knit 3 sts together.
P3tog: Purl 3 sts together.
P4tog: Purl 4 sts together.
Make Bobble (MB): [K1, p1, k1, p1, k1] into next st, making 5 sts from one; then pass 4th, 3rd, 2nd, and first st over the last st made.
Inc 2: Increase by knitting into the front, back, and then front of the same st before slipping it off the needle.

STITCH PATTERNS
Stockinette Stitch (St st)
Row 1: Knit.
Row 2: Purl.
Rep Rows 1–2 for Stockinette Stitch patt.

Tea Top Bobble Stitch (Chart A)
(over a multiple of 12 sts)
Row 1 (WS): K5, *p2, k10; rep from * to last 5 sts, k5.
Row 2 (RS): P4, *RT, LT, p8; rep from * to last 4 sts, p4.

Row 3: K the knit sts, p the purl sts.

Row 4: P2, *C3B, k2, C3F, p4; rep from * to last 2 sts, p2.

Row 5: Rep Row 3.

Row 6: P1, *2-st Right Purl Twist, p1, RT, LT, p1, 2-st Left Purl Twist, p2; rep from * to last st, p1.

Row 7: Rep Row 3.

Row 8: *2-st Right Purl Twist, p1, 2-st Right Purl Twist, k2, 2-st Left Purl Twist, p1, 2-st Left Purl Twist; rep from * across.

Row 9: Rep Row 3.

Row 10: *MB, p2tog, k1, p1, k2, p1, k1, p2tog, MB; rep from * across (60 sts).

Row 11: P1, *k1, p1, k1, p2, k1, p1, k1, p2tog; rep from * to last st, p1 (55 sts).

Row 12: P2tog, *MB, p1, k2, p1, MB, p3tog, rep from * to last 2 sts, p2tog instead of p3tog.

Row 13: K1, p1, k1, p2tog, *(k1, p1) 2 times, k1, p2tog; rep from * to last 3 sts, k1, p1, k1 (37 sts).

Row 14: *K3tog, p3tog; rep from * to last 4 sts, p4tog instead of p3tog (12 sts).

Row 15: *(K1, p1); rep from *.

Row 16: Rep Row 15.

Work Rows 1–16 once for Tea Top Bobble Stitch patt (Chart A). Bind off tightly.

Right Section Bobble Stitch (Chart B)
(over 7 sts)

Row 1 (RS): P4, RT, k1.

Row 2 (WS): K1, p2, k4.

Row 3: P2, C3F, k2.

Row 4: K1, (p1, k2) 2 times.

Row 5: P1, 2-st Right Purl Twist, p1, 2-st Right Purl Twist, k1

Row 6: (K2, p1) 2 times, k1.

Row 7: P1, MB, p2, k1, p1, k1.

Row 8: K2, p1, k4.

Row 9: P3, 2-st Right Purl Twist, p1, k1.

Row 10: K3, p1, k3.

Row 11: P2, 2-st Right Purl Twist, p1, k2.

Row 12: K1, (p1, k2) 2 times.

Row 13: P2, MB, p2, k2.

Row 14: K1, p1, k5.

Left Section Bobble Stitch (Chart C)
(over 7 sts)

Row 1 (RS): K1, LT, p4.

Row 2 (WS): K4, p2, k1.

Row 3: K2, C3B, p2.

Row 4: (K2, p1) 2 times, k1.

Row 5: K1, 2-st Left Purl Twist, p1, 2-st Left Purl Twist, p1.

Row 6: K1, (p1, k2) 2 times.

Row 7: K1, p1, k1, p2, MB, p1.

Row 8: K4, p1, k2.

Row 9: K1, p1, 2-st Left Purl Twist, p3.

Row 10: K3, p1, k3.

Row 11: K2, p1, 2-st Left Purl Twist, p2.

Row 12: (K2, p1) 2 times, k1.

Row 13: K2, p2, MB, p2.

Row 14: K5, p1, k1.

TEA COZY
Tea Top

CO 72 sts. Begin Tea Top Bobble Stitch patt (Chart A), working Rows 1–16 once. BO all sts tightly. Seam side edges to form a circle and set aside.

Handle

CO 14 sts.

Row 1 (WS): K5, p4, k5.

Row 2 (RS): P4, RT, k2, LT, p4.

Row 3 K4, p6, k4.

Row 4: P2, C3B, k4, C3F, p2.

Row 5: K2, p1, k2, p4, k2, p1, k2.

Row 6: P1, 2-st Right Purl Twist, p1, 2-st Right Purl Twist, k2, (2-st Left Purl Twist, p1) 2 times.

Row 7: K1, p1, k2, p1, k4, p1, k2, p1, k1.

Row 8 (RS): P1, MB, p2, k1, p1, k1. Turn.

Place RH needle sts on spare needle or cable needle (Left Section sts).

Right Side of Handle

Beg on WS, work Rows 8–14, then Rows 1–7 of Right Section Bobble Stitch (Chart B). Leave 7 sts on spare needle or cable needle. Cut yarn.

Left Side of Handle

Place Left Section sts from cable or spare needle (7 sts) onto LH needle. Reattach yarn on RS. Work Rows 7–14, then Rows 1–8 of Left Section Bobble Stitch (Chart C).

Joining Right and Left Handle Stitches

With WS facing, slip right section sts onto LH needle, k2, p1, k4 (14 sts).

Turn.

Next Row (RS): P3, 2-st Right Purl Twist, p1, k2, p1, 2-st Left Purl Twist, p3.

Next Row: K3, p1, k6, p1, k3.
BO all sts.

Spout
CO 14 sts. Work as for Handle until Joining Right and Left Handle Stitches.

Joining Right and Left Side Spout Stitches
Slip right section sts onto LH needle, k2, p1, k4.
Turn.
Next Row (RS): P3, 2-st Right Purl Twist, p1, k2, p1, 2-st Left Purl Twist, p3.
BO all sts.

Panel
CO 86 sts. Work in St st until piece measures 10"/23cm.
BO all sts. Weave in ends. Felt the panel.

FELTING
It generally takes 10 to 15 minutes to felt the fabric. Check fabric frequently during felting and stop the process when fabric has shrunk to desired size. The outer edge will be looser than the rest of the fabric. The felted fabric should have dimensions of at least 5 x 22½"/11.4 x 57.2cm.

Drying the Felt
Lay fabric on flat surface to dry.

Cutting the Felt
Cut 2 pieces of felt the same size, following measurements in schematic.

FINISHING AND ASSEMBLY
1. Cut 2 pieces of felt according to measurements in the schematic.
2. Cut out a heart shape in the center of first felt panel, as shown in instructions under Cutting and Finishing the Heart.
3. Thread embroidery needle with yellow floss. Chain-stitch the word "Tea" on the second felt panel as shown in the schematic.
4. Attach knitted Spout and Handle panels to sides of felted panels. Whipstitch on WS, completing Body.
5. Attach knitted Tea Top to Body, whipstitching on WS.
6. Attach a ruffled bell edging to bottom of base according to instructions under Ruffle Bell Edging.
7. Weave in ends.
8. Slip cozy over teapot, first inserting handle into opening, then inserting the spout.

Cutting and Finishing the Heart
1. Cut the heart in the center of one panel according to heart template measurements.
2. Using embroidery floss in the same color as felt, thread embroidery needle and work running stitch around WS of heart to reinforce edges.
3. Weave in ends.

Ruffle Bell Edging
Pick up 104 sts around bottom of tea cozy by poking through bottom edge of tea cozy. Pm at beg of rnd and join, being careful not to twist sts. Knit 1 rnd.
Next Rnd: Inc 2 stitches in each st around (312 sts). Knit 3 rnds.
Next Rnd: K1,* BO 8 sts, pass first knit st over BO st on RH needle, BO 3 sts; rep from * to last 4 sts. BO remaining 4 sts.

DESIGN TIP
If you have leftover yarn, knit and felt a matching cozy for your teacup.

STITCH PATTERN CHARTS

Tea Top Bobble Stitch
(Chart A)

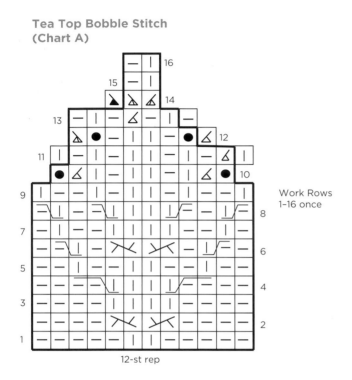

Work Rows
1–16 once

12-st rep

Legend

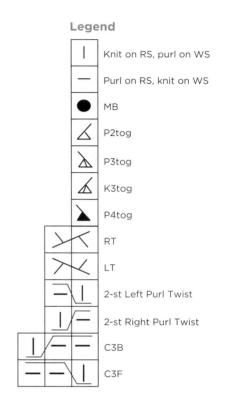

|	Knit on RS, purl on WS
—	Purl on RS, knit on WS
●	MB
P2tog symbol	P2tog
P3tog symbol	P3tog
K3tog symbol	K3tog
▲	P4tog
RT symbol	RT
LT symbol	LT
2-st Left Purl Twist symbol	2-st Left Purl Twist
2-st Right Purl Twist symbol	2-st Right Purl Twist
C3B symbol	C3B
C3F symbol	C3F

Left Section Bobble Stitch
(Chart C)

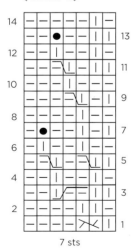

7 sts

Right Section Bobble Stitch
(Chart B)

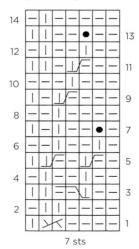

7 sts

SCHEMATICS

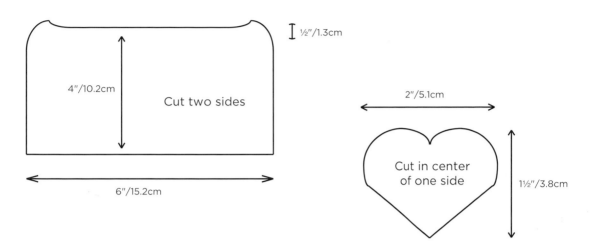

4"/10.2cm

Cut two sides

6"/15.2cm

½"/1.3cm

2"/5.1cm

Cut in center
of one side

1½"/3.8cm

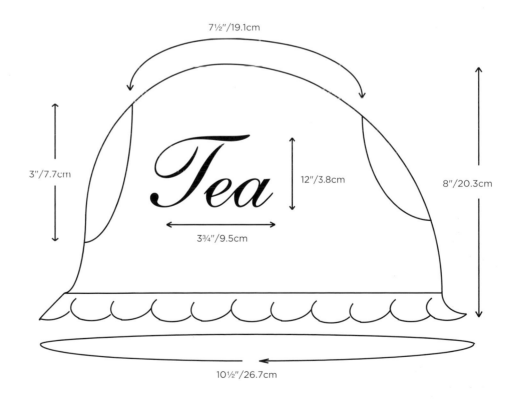

7½"/19.1cm

3"/7.7cm

Tea

12"/3.8cm

3¾"/9.5cm

8"/20.3cm

10½"/26.7cm

TOASTY TOES SLIPPERS

Mornings are a little easier to face when these felted slippers are waiting to greet your loved one. These classic slippers, featuring lovely cable panels and cheery floral-print lining, will cheer the recipient's morning and lure her away from the comfort of her bed.

SKILL LEVEL
Easy

SIZE
U.S. ladies sizes 5–10½ Extra Wide (see Shoe Size Conversion Chart for Australian, European, Japanese, UK sizes, and centimeter measurement) Shown in U.S. size 10½ Extra Wide

FINISHED MEASUREMENTS
Length: 9 to 10½"/23–26.7cm
Width: 5½ to 7½"/14–19cm

YARN
1 skein of Brown Sheep Nature Spun Worsted (100% wool, 3.5 oz/100g = 245 yd/224m per skein) in color #N03 Grey Heather OR approximately 245 yd/224m medium-weight wool yarn in light gray

MATERIALS
- Size 7 U.S. (4.5mm) and size 9 U.S. (5.5mm) needles, or size to obtain gauge
- Cable needle
- Stitch marker
- Tapestry needle
- Sewing needle and cotton thread
- Sewing machine
- Measuring tape
- Scissors
- ¼ yd (25cm) printed lining fabric of your choice
- 2 9 x 12" (23 x 31cm) sheets of Kunin Rainbow Classicfelt each in Black (#937) and Silver Gray (#928), OR two 9 x 12" (23 x 31cm) sheets of felt in black and gray
- 2 pieces (each 8½ x 11"/21.6 x 28cm) Tandy Leather Factory Cowhide Suede Trim, #4040-01, in black OR 2 pieces (each 8½ x 11"/21.6 x 28cm) black cowhide suede trim
- ¼ yd (25cm) of ½" (1.27cm)-wide foam

GAUGE
20 sts = 4"/10cm over St st using smaller needles
Always take time to check your gauge.

PATTERN NOTES
- Both chart and written instructions are provided for Toasty Toes Cable Stitch. Choose the instruction method you prefer.
- The knitted pieces are felted, cut according to template specifications, and hand- or machine-sewn together.
- For slipper construction, refer to the Finishing and Assembly instructions and accompanying diagrams.
- Foam can be purchased in the upholstery section of your local fabric store or where pillow forms are sold.
- The Shoe Size Conversion Chart provides basic measurements for ladies' shoe sizes in inches and centimeters.
- For instructions on whipstitching, see page 36.
- For instructions on felting, see page 33.

SPECIAL ABBREVIATIONS
3-st Left Twist: Slip 2 sts to cable needle and hold in front of work, p1, k2 from cable needle.

3-st Right Twist: Slip 1 st to cable needle and hold in back of work, k2, p1 from cable needle.

4-st Right Cable: Slip 2 sts to cable needle and hold in back of work, k2, k2 from cable needle.

4-st Left Cable: Slip 2 sts to cable needle and hold in front of work, k2, k2 from cable needle.

STITCH PATTERNS
Stockinette Stitch (St st)
Row 1: Knit.
Row 2: Purl.
Rep Rows 1–2 for Stockinette Stitch patt.

Toasty Toes Cable Stitch (over 17 sts)
Rows 1, 3, 5, 7, 9, and 11 (WS): K2, p2, k2, p4, k2, p2, k3.
Row 2 (RS): K2, p1, k2, p2, 4-st Right Cable, p2, k2, p1, k1.
Row 4: K2, p1, k2, p2, k4, p2, k2, p1, k1.
Row 6: Rep Row 2.
Row 8: Rep Row 4.
Row 10: Rep Row 2.

Row 12: K2, p1, (3-st Left Twist, 3-st Right Twist) 2 times, p1, k1.
Row 13: K3, p4, k2, p4, k4.
Row 14: K2, p2, 4-st Right Cable, p2, 4-st Left Cable, p2, k1.
Row 15: Rep Row 13.
Row 16: K2, p1, (3-st Right Twist, 3-st Left Twist) 2 times, p1, k1.
Rows 17 and 19: Rep Row 1.
Rows 18 and 20: Rep Row 4.
Rep Rows 1–20 for Toasty Toes Cable Stitch patt.

SLIPPERS
Cable Panel for Upper (Make 2)
With smaller needles, CO 17 sts. Beg with Row 1 (WS), work Toasty Toes Cable Stitch patt until piece measures 8"/20.3cm from cast-on edge. BO all sts.

Slipper Body
With larger needles CO 72 sts. Work in St st until piece measures 19½"/49.5cm from cast-on edge. Felt Slipper Body.

FELTING
It generally takes 10 to 15 minutes to felt the fabric. Check fabric frequently during felting and stop the process when fabric has shrunk to desired size. The outer edge will be looser than the rest of the fabric. The felted fabric should have dimensions of at least 14 x 16"/35.6 x 41cm.

MEASURING FOOT SIZE
Foot Length
Refer to the Shoe Size Conversion chart for the correct measurement to fit the recipient's shoe size.

FINISHING AND ASSEMBLY
1. Weave in ends. Block cable panel.
2. Cut lining, foam, soles, and heel support according to Cutting Diagram.
3. Cut Uppers according to Cutting Diagram. For US size 5–6½, cut 6"/15.2cm; for US size 7–8½, cut 7"/17.8cm; for US size 9–10½", cut 8"/20.3cm.
4. Whipstitch cable panel horizontally to felted Upper. Upper made.
5. On WS, machine-stitch gray craft felt lining to wrong side of Upper along sides. Set aside.
6. Place sole fabric lining over sole craft felt lining. Machine-stitch along sides. Sole lining made. RS of sole lining is fabric side.
7. Pin heel support evenly around bottom edge of sole lining. Machine-stitch along sides.
8. Pin upper to RS of sole lining around top edge. Upper will overlap ½" (0.6cm) over heel support.
9. Attach Upper by machine-stitching around top of sole lining. Slipper base made.
10. Trim edges ⅛"/0.3cm around slipper base. Set aside.
11. Machine-stitch suede sole to side sole support along edge on WS. Turn RS out. Soles made.
12. Place foam inside of soles. Place bottom of slipper base over foam.
13. Whipstitch side sole supports to slipper base, keeping a ¼"/0.6cm hem around edges.
14. Weave in ends.

DESIGN TIP
To make the slippers super-warm, line them with fur instead of fabric.

STITCH CHART

Toasty Toes Cable Stitch (over 17 sts)

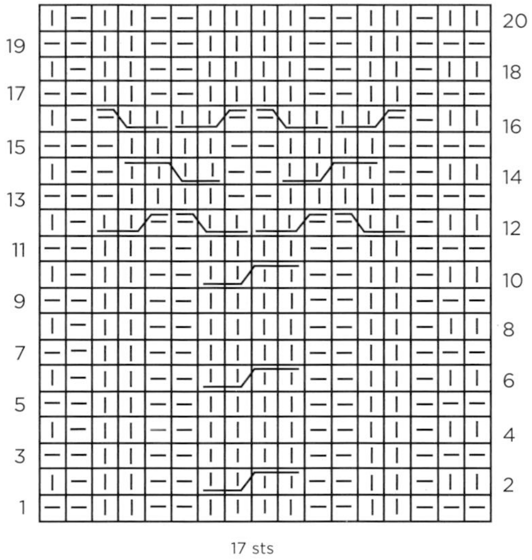
20
19
18
17
16
15
14
13
12
11
10
9
8
7
6
5
4
3
2
1
17 sts

Rep Rows 1-20

Legend

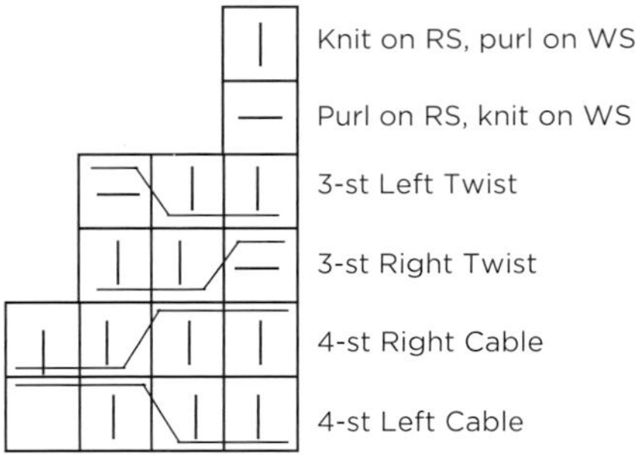
Knit on RS, purl on WS
Purl on RS, knit on WS
3-st Left Twist
3-st Right Twist
4-st Right Cable
4-st Left Cable

FINISHED MEASUREMENTS

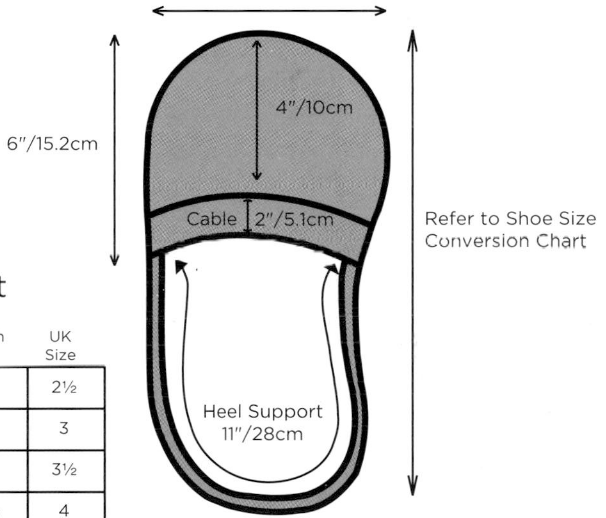
5½", 6½", 7½"/14cm, 17cm, 19cm
6"/15.2cm
4"/10cm
Cable
2"/5.1cm
Heel Support
11"/28cm
Refer to Shoe Size Conversion Chart

Shoe Size Conversion Chart

U.S. Size	Length in inches	Length in centimeters	Australia Size	Euro Size	Japan Size	UK Size
5	9"	22.8cm	3½	35	21	2½
5½	9⅛"	23.2cm	4	35½	21½	3
6	9¼"	23.5cm	4½	36	22	3½
6½	9⅜"	23.8cm	5	37	22½	4
7	9½"	24.1cm	5½	37½	23	4½
7½	9⅝"	24.4cm	6	38	23½	5
8	9¾"	24.8cm	6½	38½	24	5½
8½	9⅞"	25.1cm	7	39	24½	6
9	10"	25.4cm	7½	40	25	6½
9½	10⁶⁄₇"	25.7cm	8	41	25½	7
10	10¼"	26cm	8½	42	26	7½
10½	10½"	26.7cm	9	43	27	8

SCHEMATIC

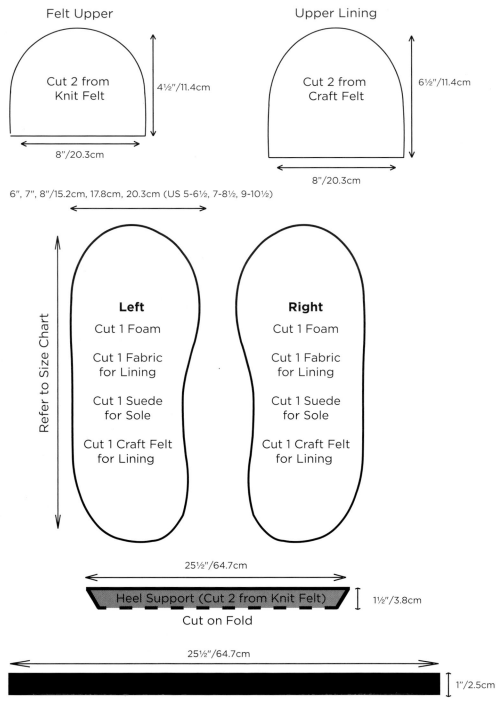

Felt Upper

Cut 2 from
Knit Felt

4½"/11.4cm

8"/20.3cm

Upper Lining

Cut 2 from
Craft Felt

6½"/11.4cm

8"/20.3cm

6", 7", 8"/15.2cm, 17.8cm, 20.3cm (US 5-6½, 7-8½, 9-10½)

Refer to Size Chart

Left

Cut 1 Foam

Cut 1 Fabric
for Lining

Cut 1 Suede
for Sole

Cut 1 Craft Felt
for Lining

Right

Cut 1 Foam

Cut 1 Fabric
for Lining

Cut 1 Suede
for Sole

Cut 1 Craft Felt
for Lining

25½"/64.7cm

Heel Support (Cut 2 from Knit Felt)

1½"/3.8cm

Cut on Fold

25½"/64.7cm

1"/2.5cm

Sole Support (Cut 2 from Craft Felt)

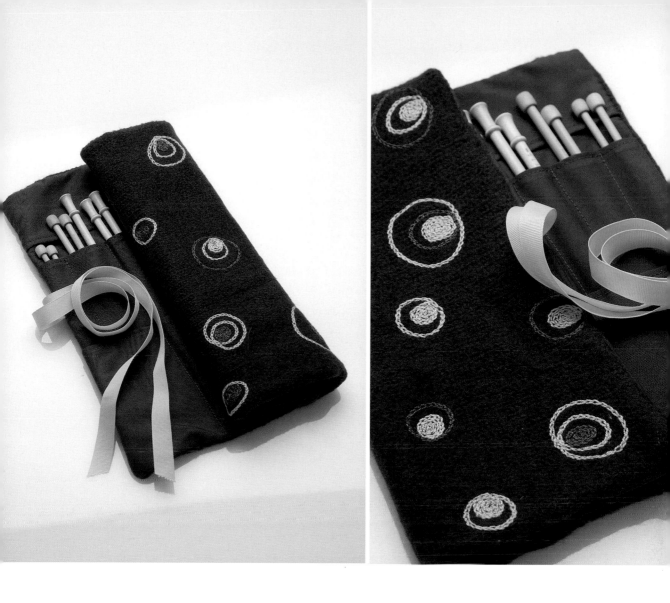

RETRO KNITTING NEEDLE CASE

Looking for the perfect gift for your favorite knitting buddy? What better gift is there than a classy case that will keep her needles in style. This felted case, knitted in rich chocolate brown and embroidered in bright colors, has a retro look. The interior lining is made to fit every important tool, keeping the knitter organized *and* trendy.

SKILL LEVEL
Easy

FINISHED MEASUREMENTS
Length: 13½"/34.3cm
Width: 16½"/42cm

YARN
1 skein of Brown Sheep Nature Spun Worsted (100% wool, 3.5 oz/100g = 245 yd/224m per skein) in color #N89W Roasted Coffee OR approximately 245 yd/224m medium-weight wool yarn in rich brown

MATERIALS
- Size 9 U.S. (5.5mm) needles, or size needed to obtain gauge
- Straight pins
- Stitch marker
- Tapestry needle
- Embroidery needle, size 22
- ½ yd (45.5cm) lining fabric of your choice
- 42" (106.7cm) of ⅝"-wide yellow ribbon, cut into 2 21" (53.3cm) lengths
- 1 skein each DMC Pearl Cotton size 5 (100% cotton, 27.3 yd/25m) in #326, #3348, and #725 OR approximately 27.3 yd/25m size 5 cotton embroidery thread in rose, light green, and topaz yellow

GAUGE
16 sts = 4"/10cm over St st
Always take time to check your gauge.

PATTERN NOTES
- The entire skein is used to knit the needle case—no yarn will remain.
- The knitted piece is felted and embroidered in chain stitch. Refer to Embroidery Diagram and photograph for placement of embroidered design.
- Individual pockets for needles and notions are created by machine-stitching the lining fabric. Refer to Lining Diagram.
- For instructions on felting, see page 33.
- For instructions on cutting out lining, see page 37.
- For instructions on whipstitching, see page 36.
- For instructions on chain stitch, see page 36.

STITCH PATTERNS
Stockinette Stitch (St st)
Row 1: Knit.
Row 2: Purl.
Rep Rows 1–2 for Stockinette Stitch patt.

KNITTING CASE
CO 72 sts. Work in St st until 2 yd/1.8m of yarn remain. BO all sts. Felt the Knitting Case as described below.

FELTING
It generally takes 10 to 15 minutes to felt the fabric. Check fabric frequently during felting and stop the process when fabric has shrunk to desired size. The outer edge will be looser than the rest of the fabric. The felted base fabric should have dimensions of at least 16½ x 13½"/42 x 34.3cm.

FINISHING AND ASSEMBLY
Decorating Knitted Felt
1. Trim sides of felted piece so that the piece forms an even rectangle.
2. Thread embroidery needle with floss. Refer to Embroidery Diagram and legend for placement of embroidered circles.
3. Weave ends into back of felt.

Cutting and Sewing Lining
1. Refer to Lining Diagram for placement of pockets.
2. Base Lining:
   *Cut out lining to match measurements of felted fabric, 16¾ x 13¾"/42.5 x 34cm.
3. Large Pocket (LP):
   *Cut out lining measuring 16¾ x 11¼"/42.5 x 28.5cm.
   *Sew hem along top of long (16¾"/42.5cm) edge of pocket.
4. Small Pocket (SP):
   *Cut out lining measuring 16¾ x 5¾"/42.5 x 14.6cm.
   *Sew hem along top of long (16¾"/42.5cm) edge of pocket.

SCHEMATIC
Embroidery Diagram

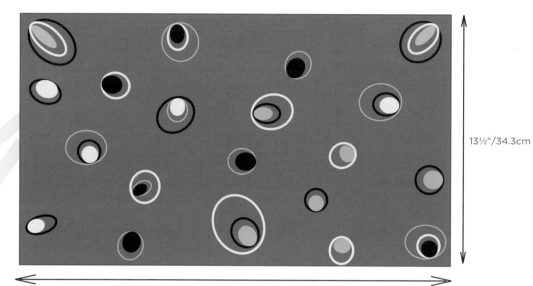

13½"/34.3cm

16½"/42cm

Legend

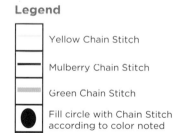

Yellow Chain Stitch

Mulberry Chain Stitch

Green Chain Stitch

Fill circle with Chain Stitch
according to color noted

Dash signifies sewing

SCHEMATIC
Stitching of Lining Diagram

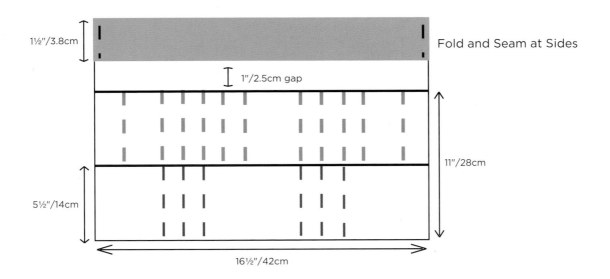

1½"/3.8cm — Fold and Seam at Sides

1"/2.5cm gap

11"/28cm

5½"/14cm

16½"/42cm

5. Needle Point Cover (NPC): *Cut out lining measuring 16¾ x 2½"/42.5 x 6.4cm. *Sew hem along long (16¾"/42.5cm) edge.
6. Place LP over bottom of base lining. Stay stitch sides.
7. Machine-stitch inner needle pockets on LP, following Lining Diagram for placement details.
8. Place SP over bottom edge of LP. Stay stitch sides.
9. Machine-stitch inner needle pockets on SP, following Lining Diagram for placement details.
10. Place NPC over top edge of base lining with hem side facing downward. Stay stitch sides.
11. Place WS of lining and WS of felted piece together (RS of both face outward).
12. Fold in raw edges of both lining and felted piece.
13. Whipstitch both sides, leaving a ½"/1.3cm gap on one side of case (refer to Embroidery Diagram). Slip edge of ribbons between felt and lining. Whipstitch to secure.
14. Weave in any loose ends.
15. Lightly press lining with iron on lowest setting.

DESIGN TIP
Use metallic embroidery floss to give your needle case a touch of shimmer.

SUMMER-DAY PLACEMAT AND NAPKIN RING

Summer is all about keeping it cool and casual, and this table setting does both. The simple stitching and the added I-cord–woven napkin ring make it an easy hostess gift for a casual summer dinner party or a trendy wedding gift for newlyweds.

SKILL LEVEL
Beginner

FINISHED MEASUREMENTS
Placemat
Length: 17"/43.2cm
Height: 13½"/34.3cm

Napkin Ring
Diameter: 2"/5.1cm

YARN
1 skein of South West Trading Company Bamboo (100% bamboo, 100g = 250 yd/228.6m per skein) in color #521-Sky OR approximately 250 yd/228.6m medium-weight bamboo yarn in sky blue

MATERIALS
- Size 6 U.S. (4mm) needles, or size needed to obtain gauge
- Straight pins
- Stitch marker
- Tapestry needle

GAUGE
22 sts = 4"/10cm over St st
Always take time to check your gauge.

PATTERN NOTES
- The placemat is worked in one piece. The cording is worked, woven, and sewn to the placemat. There are 6 I-cords—3 long and 3 short. See schematic for placing cording on placemat.
- The cording for the napkin ring is woven and joined at the ends to form a circle. There are 4 I-cords— 1 long and 3 short. See schematics for instructions.
- For instructions on working I-cord, see page 29.
- For instructions on whipstitching, see page 36.

SPECIAL ABBREVIATION
Sm: Slip marker

PLACEMAT
CO 95 sts. Knit 4 rows.
Row 5 (WS): K4, pm, purl across to last 4 sts, pm, k4.
Row 6 (RS): K4, sm, knit across to last 4 sts, sm, k4.
Rep Rows 5 and 6 until piece measures 12½"/31.8cm. Knit 4 rows.
BO all sts.

Cording for Placemat
Make a total of 6 I-cords as follows:
(Make 3 long I-cords): CO 4 sts, work in I-cord until cord measures 15½"/39.8cm. BO all sts.
(Make 3 short I-cords): CO 4 sts, work in I-cord until cord measures 12½"/31.8cm. BO all sts.

Cording for Napkin Ring
Make a total of 4 I-cords as follows:
(Make 1 long I-cord): CO 4 sts, work in I-cord until cord measures 13½"/34.2cm. BO all sts.
(Make 3 short I-cords): CO 4 sts, work in I-cord until cord measures 6"/15.2cm. BO all sts.

FINISHING AND ASSEMBLY
Placemat
1. Weave in ends.
2. Block placemat to finished measurements.
3. Arrange placemat I-cords according to placemat schematic
4. Weave I-cords vertically and horizontally as shown.
5. Secure I-cords to RS of placemat by whipstitching ends between garter st border and St st body on all 4 sides.
6. Secure I-cords to placemat base by stitching from underside of I-cord to placemat, so the I-cord will not move.
7. Weave in remaining ends.

Napkin Ring
1. Arrange 3 short I-cords horizontally as shown in the schematic.
2. Weave the long I-cord through all 3 short I-cords as shown in the schematic, making sure the weaving is even.
3. Secure ends of all I-cord edges to adjacent I-cords.
4. Join and secure ends of entire piece together to form a ring.
5. Weave in ends.

SCHEMATICS

Placemat

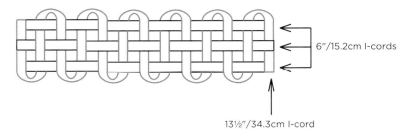

13.5"/34.3cm

8.5"/21.6cm

4"/10.2cm

15½"/39.8cm I-cords

12½"/31.8cm I-cords

17"/43.2cm

Napkin Ring I-Cord Weave

6"/15.2cm I-cords

13½"/34.3cm I-cord

DESIGN TIP
After blocking, spray the back of your work with starch to stabilize the fabric.

O-SCARF

Scarves make great presents, and this one runs circles around more traditional winter accessories. With its simple cable rib knit in vibrant colors, this project is sure to please. Uniquely designed with a circular opening, similar to a turtleneck, this scarf can simply be pulled over the head—no wrapping required, and no slipping away in the wind.

SKILL LEVEL
Easy

FINISHED MEASUREMENTS
Width: 5¼"/13.5cm
Length: 58"/147.3cm

YARN
1 skein of Mountain Colors Twizzle (85% merino wool/15% silk, 100g = 250 yd/228.6m per hank) in color Crazy Woman OR approximately 250 yd/228.6m medium-weight merino wool/silk blend yarn in multi-magenta

MATERIALS
- Size 9 U.S. (5.5mm) needles, or size needed to obtain gauge
- Tapestry needle
- Spare needle and cable needle

GAUGE
14 sts = 4"/10cm over St st
Always take time to check your gauge.

PATTERN NOTES
- Instructions are given for size S/M, with size (L) in parentheses. When only one number is given, it pertains to all sizes. Take care to follow the set of instructions that pertains to your chosen size throughout.
- The scarf is worked over 28 sts for the first 25"/ 63.5cm (24½"/62.2cm). Two layers of fabric are worked separately for 8"/20.3cm (9"/22.9cm). Finally, the 2 layers are merged, and the last part of the scarf is worked over 28 sts.
- Both chart and written instructions for O-Scarf Stitch are provided. Choose the instruction method you prefer.
- The O-Scarf is worn much like a turtleneck: just slip it over your head.

SPECIAL ABBREVIATIONS
P-inc 1: Purl into back, then into front of next st.
M1: Insert LH needle from front to back into the horizontal strand between the last st worked and the next st on LH needle. Pick up this strand and knit through the back loop.
2-st Right Purl Twist: Slip 1 st to cable needle, hold in back of work, k1, p1 from cable needle.
2-st Left Purl Twist: Slip 1 st to cable needle, hold in front of work, p1, k1 from cable needle.
Wrap2: *Bring yarn to front of work, slip 3 sts to RH needle, wrap yarn around RH needle, slip 3 sts to LH needle; rep from * once more, k3.
N1: Needle 1
N2: Needle 2
Knit 2 sts from both needles (K2N): Insert the RH needle into the first st on N1 as if to knit. Then insert the RH needle into the first st on the cable needle as if to knit. Knit these 2 sts together. Drop both sts from cable needle and N1.
Purl 2 sts from both needles (P2N): Insert the RH needle into the first st on the cable needle as if to purl. Then insert the RH needle into the first st on N1 as if to purl. Purl these 2 stitches together. Drop both sts from cable needle and N1.
Slip 3 and Wrap (S3W): *Bring yarn to front of N1, slip 3 sts of N1 to RH needle, wrap yarn around cable needle and N1 needle, slip 3 sts from RH to N1 needle; rep from * once, (K2N) 3 times.

STITCH PATTERN
O-Scarf Stitch (over 28 sts)
Row 1 (RS): K2, p2, (k1, p1) 2 times, k1, (p2, k2) 2 times, p2, (k1, p1) 2 times, k1, p2, k2.
Row 2 and all WS rows: Knit the knit sts, and purl the purl sts.
Row 3: K2, p2, 2-st Left Purl Twist, k1, 2-st Right Purl Twist, (p2, k2) 2 times, p2, 2-st Left Purl Twist, k1, 2-st Right Purl Twist, p2, k2.
Row 5: K2, p3, wrap2, p3, k2, p2, k2, p3, wrap2, p3, k2.
Row 7: K2, p2, 2-st Right Purl Twist, k1, 2-st Left Purl Twist, (p2, k2) 2 times, p2, 2-st Right

Purl Twist, k1, 2-st Left Purl Twist, p2, k2.

Row 9: Rep Row 1.

Row 10: Knit the k sts and purl the p sts.

Rep Rows 1–10 for O-Scarf Stitch patt.

SCARF

CO 28 sts. Knit 2 rows. Begin working O-Scarf Stitch patt. Cont until scarf measures 25"/63.5cm (24½"/62.2cm), ending on Row 5. Turn.

Forming Two Layers

Next Row (WS): P-inc 1, m1, p1, m1, (k1, m1) 3 times, (p1, m1) 3 times, (k1, m1) 2 times, (p1, m1) 2 times, (k1, m1) 2 times, (p1, m1) 2 times, (k1, m1) 3 times, (p1, m1) 3 times, (k1, m1) 3 times, p1, m1, P-inc 1 (56 sts).

Next Row (RS): Place first P-inc st, all m1 sts, and last P-inc 1 st on a spare needle (N2) at the back of the work.

Position of Needles

Two needles are holding the scarf: N1 holds original scarf sts, N2 holds all inc and m1 sts. With N1 in front and N2 in back, begin work on N2 with Row 7. Work patt as established until this section measures 8"/20.3cm (9"/22.9cm), ending with Row 4.

Next Row (WS): Place N2 sts on cable needle and place aside.

Reattach yarn on WS of N1 and work patt, beg with Row 7. (WS of neck section are facing.) Work in patt as established until this section measures 8"/20.3cm (9"/22.9cm), ending with Row 4.

Combining Layers

Next Row (RS): With N1 in front and cable needle in back, work Row 5 of patt by working N1 and cable needle

sts together as follows: (K2N) 2 times, (P2N) 3 times, S3W, (P2N) 3 times, [(K2N) 2 times, (P2N) 2 times] 2 times, (P2N) 3 times, S3W, (P2N) 3 times, (K2N) 2 times. Two layers are combined into one (28 sts).

Next Row (WS): Cont in patt as established until scarf measures 58"/147.3cm from beg. BO all sts.

FINISHING AND ASSEMBLY

1. Weave in ends.
2. Block scarf.

DESIGN TIP

Give your scarf a more traditional look by adding fringe. Be sure to set aside a bit of yarn for fringe before you start knitting.

SCHEMATIC

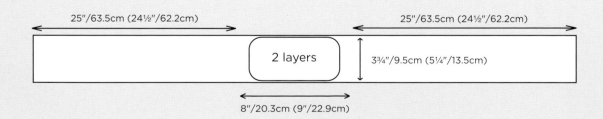

25"/63.5cm (24½"/62.2cm)   25"/63.5cm (24½"/62.2cm)

2 layers   3¾"/9.5cm (5¼"/13.5cm)

8"/20.3cm (9"/22.9cm)

STITCH CHART
O-Scarf Stitch
(over 28 sts)

Rep Rows 1-10

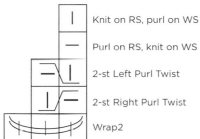

14

Legend

 Knit on RS, purl on WS

— Purl on RS, knit on WS

2-st Left Purl Twist

2-st Right Purl Twist

Wrap2

SPIRAL-VINE VASE COVER

Looking for the perfect housewarming gift? This spiral lace vase cover is an eye-catching gift that will bring a modern touch to any home décor with just one ball. Knit in mohair yarn with minimal shaping, the cover provides a perfect fit.

SKILL LEVEL
Intermediate

FINISHED MEASUREMENTS
Height: 16"/40.6cm
Width at base: 13"/33cm

YARN
1 skein of Filatura Di Crosa Baby Kid Extra (80% mohair/20% nylon, 0.87 oz/ 25g = 268 yd/245m per skein) in color #504 Light Olive OR approximately 268 yd/245m super fine-weight mohair/ nylon blend yarn in light green

MATERIALS
• Size 8 U.S. (5mm) needles, or size needed to obtain gauge
• Stitch marker
• Tapestry needle
• Wooden vase 15½"/39.4cm tall

GAUGE
16 sts = 4"/10cm in St st using two strands of yarn held together
Always take time to check your gauge.

PATTERN NOTES
• Use 2 strands of yarn held together throughout the pattern.
• Both chart and written instructions for the Petite Petal Lace Stitch are provided. Choose the instruction method you prefer.

• The piece is wide at the base and narrow at the top, conforming to the shape of the vase.
• The piece is worked flat and seamed at the sides, forming a circular tube.
• Pull the knitted tube over the vase.
• For instructions on mattress stitch, refer to page 35.

SPECIAL ABBREVIATIONS.
K3tog: Knit 3 sts together.
P3tog: Purl 3 sts together.
P5tog: Purl 5 sts together.
Make bobble (MB): [K1, p1, k1, p1, k1] into next st; then pass 5th, 4th, 3rd, 2nd, and first st over the last st made.
Yo: Yarn over.

STITCH PATTERNS
Stockinette Stitch (St st)
Row 1 (RS): Knit across.
Row 2 (WS): Purl across.
Rep Rows 1 and 2 for St st patt.

Petite Petal Lace Stitch (over 28 sts + 1)
Row 1: *K5, k2tog, yo, k1, yo, skp, k18, rep from * to last st, k1.
Row 2 and all WS rows: Purl.
Row 3: *K3, (k2tog, yo) 2 times, k1, (yo, skp) 2 times, k16, rep from * to last st, k1.
Row 5: *K2, (k2tog, yo) 2 times, k3, (yo, skp) 2 times, k15, rep from * to last st, k1.
Row 7: Rep Row 3.

Row 9: *K7, MB, k20, rep from * to last st, k1.
Row 11: *K19, k2tog, yo, k1, yo, skp, k4, rep from * to last st, k1.
Row 13: *K17, (k2tog, yo) 2 times, k1, (yo, skp) 2 times, k2, rep from * to last st, k1.
Row 15: K16, (k2tog, yo) 2 times, k3, (yo, skp) 2 times, k1, rep from * to last st, k1.
Row 17: Rep Row 13.
Row 19: *K21, MB, k6, rep from * to last st, k1.
Row 20: Purl.
Rep Rows 1–20 2 times for Petite Petal Lace Stitch patt.

VASE
Unwind half the ball and cut yarn, dividing it into 2 equal balls.
Holding 2 strands of yarn together, CO 57 sts. Work Set-up Rows as follows.
Set-up Row 1: Knit.
Set-up Row 2: Purl.
Work Rows 1–20 of Petite Petal Lace Stitch patt 2 times.
Row 41 (RS): Knit.
Row 42 (WS): Purl.
Rep Rows 41 and 42 3 more times.

Shaping Top of Vase
Row 49 (RS): Knit.
Row 50 (WS): *P7, p3tog, rep from * to last 7 sts, p7 (47 sts).
Row 51: Knit.
Row 52: Purl.
Row 53: K6, *k3tog, k5; rep from * to last 6 sts, k6. (37 sts)
Row 54: P5, *p5tog, p3; rep from * to last 5 sts, p5 (27 sts).

SCHEMATICS

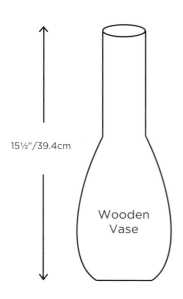

15½"/39.4cm

Wooden
Vase

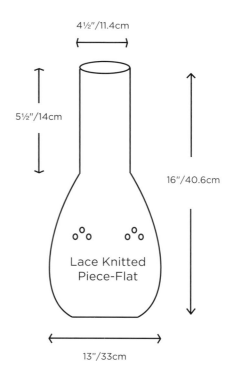

4½"/11.4cm

5½"/14cm

16"/40.6cm

Lace Knitted
Piece-Flat

13"/33cm

Row 55: K4, *k3tog, k5; rep from * to last 4 sts, k4 (21 sts). Work in St st over rem 21 sts until piece measures 16"/40.6cm from cast-on edge. BO loosely.

FINISHING AND ASSEMBLY

1. Stitch side (long) edges of knitted piece using mattress stitch to form a tube.
2. Slip knitted piece over vase.
3. Thread tapestry needle with yarn and weave along top circular edge of knitted fabric. Pull tight to secure around vase lip. Repeat for base edge.
4. Weave in all ends.

DESIGN TIP

If your vase is white, try this pattern in crimson or black for a graphic, modern look.

STITCH CHART
Petite Petal Lace Stitch
(over 28 sts + 1)

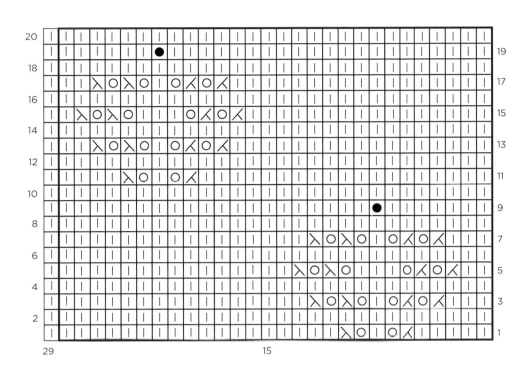

Rep Rows 1-20
2 times

Legend

|	Knit on RS, purl on WS
O	Yarn over
⋋	K2tog
⋌	Skp
●	Make Bobble

LITTLE RED DRIVING GLOVES

For the roadster in your life! These fun driving gloves, with deerskin suede on both the palms and backs for maximum grip and style, will look great whether she drives a sports car or a minivan. The wool-blend yarn contains aloe vera and jojoba oil, which soften hands and give comfort on cold winter days.

SKILL LEVEL
Easy

SIZE
Medium Adult

FINISHED MEASUREMENTS
Hand circumference: 8"/20.3cm

YARN
1 skein of Austermann Step Classic Sock (75%wool/25% nylon, 100g = 460 yd/429m per skein) in color #1005 Raspberry OR approximately 200 yd/183m fingering-weight wool/nylon blend yarn in raspberry

MATERIALS
- Size 4 U.S. (3.5mm) needles, or size to obtain gauge
- ½ yd (45cm) Tandy Leather Factory Genuine DeerSkin Red #9301-09 OR ½ yd (45cm) red deerskin
- Stitch marker
- Tapestry needle
- 1 stitching awl for punching holes in leather
- 1 skein DMC pearl cotton size 5 (100% cotton, 27.3 yd/25m) in #321 red OR approximately 27.3 yd/25m size 5 cotton embroidery thread in red

GAUGE
24 sts = 4"/10cm over St st. Always take time to check your gauge.

PATTERN NOTES
- Side Edge Knits and Side Edge Purls (see Special Abbreviations below) will close holes in the gloves. Some gaps will be closed by weaving in ends.
- For instructions on grafting, see page 31.

SPECIAL ABBREVIATIONS
Cast on 2 sts (CO2): *Knit 1 st without dropping worked st from LH needle. Slip st from RH needle to LH needle. Rep from * once more. 2 sts made.
Sm: Slip marker.
Inc 1-B: Knit into bar behind next st, knit next st. (1 st inc made).
Side Edge Knit (SEK): Place RH needle flat over LH needle, notice how sts are met side by side. Lift one left-side edge st of a previous row below st on RH needle. Lift one right-side edge of a row below stitch on LH needle. Place both side sts on LH needle, k2tog (1 st made).
Side Edge Purl (SEP): Turn work to RS. Place RH needle flat over LH needle, notice how sts are met side by side. Turn back to WS. Lift one left-side edge st of a previous row below stitch on RH needle. Lift one right-side edge st of a previous row below st on LH needle. Place both side sts on LH needle, p2tog (1 st made).

STITCH PATTERNS
Stockinette Stitch (St st)
Row 1 (RS): Knit across.
Row 2 (WS): Purl across.
Rep Rows 1 and 2 for St st patt.

Cuff Rib Stitch
Row 1 (RS): *K2, p2; rep from * across to last 2 sts, k2.
Row 2 (WS): *P2, k2; rep from * to last 2 sts, p2.
Rep Rows 1–2 for Cuff Rib Stitch patt.

GLOVES
Right Glove

Cuff
CO 50 sts. Work Cuff Rib Stitch for 2¾"/7cm, ending with WS row.

Thumb Gusset
Work in St st for 6 rows.
Row 1 (RS): K27, pm, (Inc 1-B) 2 times, pm, k21 (52 stitches).
Row 2: Purl.
Row 3: Knit.
Row 4: Purl.
Row 5: K27, sm, Inc 1-B, knit to 1 st before marker, Inc 1-B, k21. Rep Rows 2–5 until there are 12 sts between markers. Work in St st for 5 rows, end with WS row.

Thumb
Next Row (RS): Knit 39 sts. Turn.
Next Row (WS): Cast on 1 st. Purl 13 sts up to marker including cast-on st (13 sts). Turn.

Next Row (RS): Cast on 2 sts. K15 sts including cast-on sts (15 sts).

Work over these 15 sts in St st until thumb measures 1¾"/4.5cm from cast-on edge of thumb, ending with WS row.

Close Tip of Thumb

Next Row (RS): *K2tog, k1; rep from * across (10 sts).

Next Row (WS): (P2tog) 5 times (5 sts).

Cut yarn, leaving 10"/25.4cm tail. Thread tapestry needle with yarn tail and thread through all 5 sts. Slip through all 5 sts again, then use remaining tail to graft inner edges of thumb from tip to thumb cast-on edge. (1 thumb made).

Center of Hand

Next Row (RS): With RS facing, attach yarn and pick up 3 sts on cast-on edge of thumb, SEK, knit to end.

Next Row (WS): P24, SEP, purl across (53 sts).

Work 1½"/3.8cm in St st over 53 sts, ending with WS row.

Index Finger

Row 1 (RS): Knit 34 sts. Turn work.

Row 2 (WS): CO 1 st, purl 16 sts including cast-on st. Turn work.

Row 3: CO 1 st, knit across 17 sts including cast-on st. Turn work.

Work in St st over 17 sts for 2½"/6.4cm from beg of index finger, ending with WS row.

Index Finger Shaping

Next Row (RS): K4, k2tog, k5, k2tog, k4 (15 sts).

Next Row: Purl.

Next Row: Knit.

Next Row: Purl.

Next Row (RS): *K2tog, k1; rep from * across (10 sts).

Next Row (WS): (P2tog) 5 times (5 sts).

Cut yarn, leaving 10"/25.4cm tail. Work as for Close Tip of Thumb, grafting from fingertip to cast-on edge.

Middle Finger

Next Row (RS): With RS facing, attach yarn and pick up 2 sts from cast-on base of index finger, SEK, k7 sts. Turn work.

Next Row (WS): CO 1 st, p8 including cast-on st, p2tog, p1, SEP, p7. Turn work.

Next Row (RS): CO 1 st, k7 including cast-on st, k2tog, k10. Turn work. Work over 18 sts for 2½"/6.4cm from beg of middle finger cast-on edge, ending with WS row.

Shape and Close Tip of Middle Finger

Next Row (RS): K4, k2tog, k6, k2tog, k4.

Work over 16 sts until finger measures 3"/7.6cm.

Next Row (RS): *K2tog, k1; rep from * to last 2 sts, k2tog (10 sts).

Next Row (WS): (P2tog) 5 times (5 sts).

Cut yarn, leaving 10"/25.4cm tail. Work as for Close Tip of Thumb, grafting from finger tip to cast-on edge.

Ring Finger

Next Row (RS): With RS facing, attach yarn and pick up 2 sts from cast-on base of middle finger, SEK, k6. Turn work.

Next Row (WS): CO 1 st, p7 including cast-on st, p2tog, SEP, p6. Turn work.

Next Row: CO 1 st, k7 including cast-on st, k2tog, k8 (16 sts). Turn work.

Work over 16 sts for 2½"/6.4cm from beg of ring finger cast-on edge, ending with WS row.

Shape and Close Tip of Ring Finger

Next Row (RS): K4, k2tog, k4, k2tog, k4 (14 sts).

Next Row: Purl.

Next Row: Knit.

Next Row: Purl.

Next Row: *K2tog, k1; rep from * to last 2 sts, k2 (10 sts).

Next Row: (P2tog) 5 times. Cut yarn, leaving 10"/25.4cm tail. Work as for Close Tip of Thumb, grafting from finger tip to cast-on edge.

Pinky (Little Finger)

Next Row (RS): With RS facing, attach yarn and pick up 2 sts from cast-on base of ring finger, SEK, k6. Turn work.

Next Row (WS): P6, p2tog, p1, SEP, p6. Turn work.
Next Row (RS): K6, k2tog, k7. Turn work.
Work over 14 sts for 1½"/3.8cm from beg of pinky finger, ending with WS row.

Shape and Close Tip of Pinky (Little) Finger
Next Row: K4, k2tog, k2, k2tog, k4 (12 sts).
Next Row: Purl.
Next Row: *K2tog, k1; rep from * across (8 sts).
Next Row: (P2tog) 4 times (4 sts).
Cut yarn, leaving 10"/25.4cm tail. Thread tapestry needle with yarn tail and thread through all 5 sts. Slip through first 4 sts again. Do not graft sides of finger to cuff: leave open for later finishing.

Left Glove
Cast on 50 sts. Work Cuff Rib Stitch patt for 2¾"/7cm, end on WS row.

Thumb Gusset
Work in St st for 6 rows, ending on WS.
Row 1 (RS): K21, pm, (Inc 1-B) 2 times, pm, k27 (52 stitches).
Row 2: Purl.
Row 3: Knit.
Row 4: Purl.
Row 5: K21, sm, Inc 1-B, knit to one stitch before marker, Inc 1-B, k27.
Rep Rows 2–5 until there are 12 sts between marker. Work in

St st for 5 rows, ending with WS.

Thumb
Next Row (RS): K33. Turn work.
Next Row (WS): CO 2 st. P14 including cast-on sts (14 sts). Turn work.
Next Row (RS): CO 1 st. K15, including cast-on st (15 sts). Work over these 15 sts in St st for 1¾"/4.5cm from cast-on edge of thumb ending with WS row.
Work as for Close Tip of Thumb of Right Hand Glove.

Center of Hand
Next row (RS): With RS facing, pick up 3 sts on cast-on edge of thumb, SEK, knit to end.
Next Row (WS): P31, SEP, purl across (53 sts).
Work 1½"/3.8cm in St st over 53 sts, ending with WS row. Work remaining steps as for Right Glove.

FINISHING AND ASSEMBLY
1. Weave in ends, closing all holes and tightening loose sts.
2. Keep sides of gloves unstitched.
3. Block gloves.
4. Make paper templates: Trace hands on paper, adding a ⅛"/0.3cm border around hands and sides of fingers. Add a ½"/3.2cm border at the tips of all

fingers except for thumb. Rep for palm of hand by tracing the palm and thumb only.
5. Pin paper templates to leather, cutting out 1 piece each for the back of the hand and the palm. Rep for other hand, reversing template if front and back of leather have a different appearance. Refer to Cutting Template as a guide.
6. Using awl, punch holes ⅛"/0.3cm apart around edge of leather pieces.
7. Slip paper template for back of hand inside of glove. This will act as a guard, preventing accidental stitching through the other side of glove when attaching leather trim.
8. Thread tapestry needle with embroidery thread.
9. Attach leather trim to knitted glove by backstitching through holes formed with the awl. Repeat for other hand. **Note:** Backstitch by pulling thread up through knitted glove and 2nd hole on leather trim. Pull thread down through front of work and through the first hole. Skip 2nd hole worked and pull thread up through knitted glove and through the 3rd hole. Pull thread down again through

CUTTING TEMPLATE

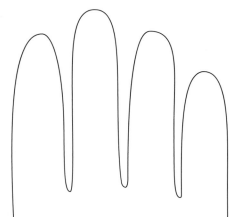

Sew on back of glove hand.

Trace your palm and four fingers.
Add a ⅛"/ 3.2cm extra border around
palm, sides, and between fingers.
Add a ½"/1.3cm extra border
on top of fingertip. Cut.

Cut 2 pieces on leather, one for left
and right hand.
Reverse template for left hand.

Sew on palm and
thumb of glove.

Trace your palm and thumb.
Add a ⅛"/ 3.2cm extra border
around palm and sides.
Add a ½"/1.3cm extra border
on top of thumb tip.

Cut 2 pieces on leather, one for left
and one for right hand.
Reverse template for left hand.

the 2nd hole worked.
Backstitch made. Rep
throughout work.
10. Remove templates from
    inside of gloves.
11. Seam sides of glove.
    Repeat for other hand.
12. Weave in ends.

DESIGN TIP
Personalize this gift by
punching out initials on the
leather pieces for the backs of
the hands.

CUDDLE-ME BABY HOODIE

Is there anything more satisfying than knitting for the adorable little tot in your life? How about a hooded sweater featuring twisted stitches and bobbles, all knit from one ball of super-soft yarn? Beginners will find this quick-knit project, adorned with bobble buttons, both endearing and baby-safe. This gift is sure to be Mom's favorite for years to come.

SKILL LEVEL
Easy

FINISHED MEASUREMENTS
Sizes 3-6 (12, 18) months
Chest: 27 (29, 30)"/68.6 (73.6, 76.2)cm
Shown in size 18 months.

YARN
1 skein of Lion Brand Yarns Babysoft (60% acrylic/40% nylon), 5 oz/140g = 459 yd/420m per skein) in color #099 Cream OR approximately 459 yd/420m lightweight acrylic/nylon blend yarn in off-white

MATERIALS
• Size 8 U.S. (5mm) needles, or size to obtain gauge
• Tapestry needle
• Stitch holder OR spare needle
• Stitch markers

GAUGE
20 sts = 4"/10cm over St st
Always take time to check your gauge.

PATTERN NOTES
• Both chart and written instructions for the Bobble and Twist Stitches are provided. Choose the instruction method you prefer.
• For instructions on three-needle bind-off, refer to page 27.

For instructions on whip-stiching, refer to page XX.

SPECIAL ABBREVIATIONS
RT: K2tog, leaving both sts on needle; insert RH needle between 2 sts, and knit first st again; slip both sts from needle.
LT: Skip the first st on LH needle and knit 2nd st through back loop, insert RH needle into backs of both sts, k2tog tbl.
MB: (Make Bobble) [K1, p1, k1, p1, k1, p1, k1] into next st, making 7 sts from one; then pass 6th, 5th, 4th, 3rd, 2nd, and first st over the last st made.
Sm: Slip marker.
Spp: Slip 1 st, purl next st. Pass the slipped st over the purl st and off the needle.
Inc 1: Inc by knitting into front and back of same st.

STITCH PATTERNS
Stockinette Stitch (St st)
Row 1: Knit.
Row 2: Purl.
Rep Rows 1–2 for Stockinette Stitch patt.

Seed Stitch
Row 1: *K1, p1; rep from * across to last st, k1.
Row 2: Purl the knit sts, and knit the purl sts.
Rep Row 2 for Seed Stitch patt.

Rib Stitch
Row 1: *K1, p1; rep from * across.
Row 2: Purl the purl sts, and knit the knit sts.
Rep Row 2 for Rib Stitch patt.

Cuddle-Me Bobble Stitch (over 15 sts)
Row 1 (RS): (LT) 3 times, k3, (RT) 3 times.
Row 2 and all WS rows: Purl.
Row 3: K1, (LT) 3 times, k1, (RT) 3 times, k1.
Row 5: (LT) 3 times, k1, MB, k1, (RT) 3 times.
Row 7: (RT) 3 times, k3, (LT) 3 times.
Row 9: K1, (RT) 3 times, k1, (LT) 3 times, k1.
Row 11: (RT) 3 times, k1, MB, k1, (LT) 3 times.
Row 12: Rep Row 2.
Rep Rows 1–12 for Cuddle-Me Bobble Stitch patt.

Cuddle-Me Twist Stitch (over 15 sts)
Row 1 (RS): (LT) 3 times, k3, (RT) 3 times.
Row 2 and all WS rows: Purl.
Row 3: K1, (LT) 3 times, k1, (RT) 3 times, k1.
Row 5: (LT) 3 times, k3, (RT) 3 times.
Row 7: (RT) 3 times, k3, (LT) 3 times.
Row 9: K1, (RT) 3 times, k1, (LT) 3 times, k1.
Row 11: (RT) 3 times, k3, (LT) 3 times.
Row 12: Rep Row 2.
Rep Rows 1–12 for Cuddle–Me Twist Stitch patt.

Cuddle-Me Right Stitch
(over 7 sts)
Row 1: K1, (RT) 3 times.
Row 2 and all WS rows: P6, k1.
Row 3: K2, (RT) 2 times, k1.
Row 5: Rep Row 1.
Row 7: K1, (LT) 3 times.
Row 9: K2, (LT) 2 times, k1.
Row 11: Rep Row 7.
Row 12: Rep Row 2.
Rep Rows 1–12 for Cuddle-Me Right Stitch patt.

Cuddle-Me Left Stitch
(over 7 sts)
Row 1 (RS): (LT) 3 times, k1.
Row 2 and all WS rows: K1, p6.
Row 3: K1, (LT) 2 times, k2.
Row 5: Rep Row 1.
Row 7: (RT) 3 times, k1.
Row 9: K1, (RT) 2 times, k2.
Row 11: Rep Row 7.
Row 12: Rep Row 2.
Rep Rows 1–12 for Cuddle-Me Left Stitch patt.

HOODIE BODY
CO 61 (67, 71) sts.
Row 1 (RS): *K1, p1; rep from * across to last st, k1.
Work 3 rows in Seed st.
Row 5 (RS): Work 4 sts in Seed st, pm, k19 (22, 24), pm, work Row 1 of Cuddle-Me Bobble Stitch patt, pm, k19 (22, 24), pm, work 4 sts in Seed st.
Row 6 (WS): Work 4 sts in Seed st, sm, p19 (22, 24), sm, work Row 2 of Cuddle-Me Bobble Stitch patt, sm, p19 (22, 24), sm, work 4 sts in Seed st.

Work in patt as established until piece measures 5½"/ 14cm from cast-on edge, ending with Row 6.

Front Opening
Next Row (RS): Work 4 sts in Seed st, k19 (22, 24), (RT) 3 times, k3, pass 2nd worked st on RH needle over just worked st (center st bound off), (LT) 3 times, k19 (22, 24) sts, work 4 sts in Seed st [60 (66, 70) sts].

Right Front
Next Row (WS): Work 4 sts in Seed st, p19 (22, 24), work Row 8 of Cuddle-Me Right Stitch.
Turn work. Work over these 30 (33, 35) sts until Right Front measures 6½ (7, 7½)"/ 16.5 (17.8, 19)cm, ending with WS row.

Sleeve Placement
Next Row (RS): Work first 7 sts in patt as established, knit across.
Next Row (WS): Purl across to last 7 sts, work 7 sts in patt.
Work in patt as established until front measures 8 (9, 10)"/20.3 (22.8, 25.4)cm, ending with WS row.

Neck Shaping
Next Row (RS): Bind off 6 sts, knit across.
Next Row (WS): Purl.
Next Row (RS): Skp, knit across.
Rep last two rows 3 more times.

Work in patt as established until piece measures 10 (11, 12)"/25.4 (27.9, 30.5)cm, ending with WS row.
Place remaining sts on stitch holder or spare needle. Break yarn.

Left Front
Reattach yarn at neck edge. Beg with Row 8 (WS) of Cuddle-Me Left Stitch, purl across 19 (22, 24) sts, work Seed st.
Work in patt as established until piece measures 6½ (7, 7½)"/ 16.5 (17.8, 19)cm, ending with WS row.

Sleeve Placement
Next Row (RS): Knit across to last 7 sts, work 7 sts in patt as established.
Next Row (WS): Work 7 sts in patt, purl across.
Work in patt as established until piece measures 8 (9, 10)"/20.3 (22.8, 25.4)cm; end with RS row.

Neck Shaping
Next Row (WS): Bind off 6 sts, purl across.
Next Row (RS): Knit.
Next Row (WS): Spp, purl across.
Rep last 2 rows 3 more times.
Work in patt as established until piece measures 10 (11, 12)"/25.4 (27.9, 30.5)cm, ending with RS row. Turn.

Back

Next Row (WS): CO 21 sts, purl across cast-on sts and all rem stitches of Left Front [41 (44, 46) sts].

Next Row (RS): Knit across 41 (44, 46) sts and all 20 (23, 25) sts of Right Front.

Cont to work in St st until back measures 3½ (4, 4½)"/9 (10, 11.4) cm, ending with a WS row [61 (67, 71) sts].

Next Row (RS): (K1, p1) 2 times, k53 (59, 63), (p1, k1) 2 times.

Next Row (WS): Work 4 sts in Seed st, p53 (59, 63), work 4 sts in Seed st.

Cont in patt until back measures 9½ (10½, 11½)"/24.1 (26.7, 29.2) cm from cast-on sts. Work 4 rows in Seed st. BO all sts.

SLEEVES

Right Sleeve

With RS facing, pick up and knit 37 (41, 47) sts along the St st edge of right side of body between Seed st borders.

Row 1 (WS): Purl.

Row 2: K11 (13, 16), pm, work Row 1 of Cuddle-Me Twist Stitch, pm, k11 (13, 16).

Row 3: Spp, purl to last 2 sts, k2tog.

Row 4: K10 (12, 15), work Row 2 of Cuddle-Me Twist Stitch, k10 (12, 15).

Row 5: Purl.

Row 6: Skp, k8 (10, 13) sts,

work Row 3 of Cuddle-Me Twist, k8 (10, 13), k2tog.

Cont to work as established, dec 1 st at each end every 4th (3rd, 3rd) row until 31 sts rem. Work in patt as established with no further decreases until sleeve measures 4 (4½, 5)"/10 (11.4, 12.7) cm, ending with WS row.

Cuff Shaping

Next Row (RS): K1, p1, k1, p2tog, (k1, p1) 2 times, k2tog, p1, k1, p1, k2tog, (p1, k1) 2 times, p2tog, k1, p1, k1, p2tog, (k1, p1) 2 times (26 sts)

Work in Rib st until sleeve measures 5½ (6, 6½)"/14 (15.2, 16.5) cm. BO all sts.

Left Sleeve

Work as for Right Sleeve.

Hood

Using a removable stitch holder or scrap yarn, mark the center back sts. With RS facing, pick up and knit 25 sts along right neck edge, shoulder, and back, up to the marker, pm. Pick up 25 sts along rest of back, shoulder, and left neck edge (50 sts). Turn.

Next Row (WS): (K1, p1) 2 times, purl across to last 4 sts, (k1, p1) 2 times.

Next Row (RS): Work 4 sts in Seed st, knit across to last 4 sts, work 4 sts in Seed st. Rep these 2 rows until hood measures 2"/5.1cm, ending

with WS row.

Next Row (RS): Work first 24 sts as established, inc 1, sm, inc 1, work rem sts as established.

Cont in patt, inc 1 st on each side of marker every 4th row 5 mores times (62 sts). Work even for 3 rows, ending with WS row.

Shaping Hood

Next Row (RS): Work 4 sts in Seed st, k25, skp, sm, k2tog, k25, work 4 sts in Seed st. Dec every 3rd (4th, 4th) row until 56 sts remain. Work 2 rows even, ending with RS row. *For smallest size, substitute p2tog and spp when decreases fall on WS rows.*

Three-Needle Bind-Off for Hood

Turn. With WS facing, slip 28 sts onto a spare needle. Fold the hood sts on the 2 needles so the RSs are facing and the needles are parallel (28 sts on each needle). With 3rd needle, knit together the first st on each needle. *(Work the next st on each needle in the same way. You now have 2 sts on the RH needle. Lift the first st over the 2nd st and off needle; rep from * to end. Cut yarn and slip yarn through last st to secure. Turn hood RS out.

Bobble Buttons (Make 4)

CO 1 st, leaving 2"/5.1cm tail. [K1, p1, k1, p1, k1, p1, k1] into

CHARTS

Cuddle-Me Bobble Stitch

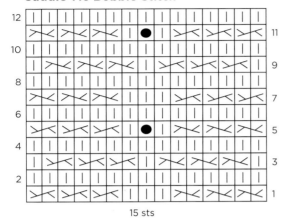

15 sts

Cuddle-Me Twist Stitch

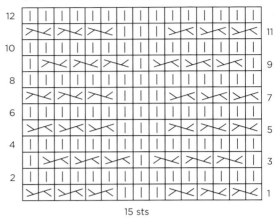

15 sts

Cuddle-Me Right Stitch

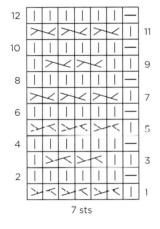

7 sts

Cuddle-Me Left Stitch

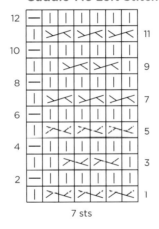

7 sts

Legend

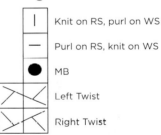

	Knit on RS, purl on WS
—	Purl on RS, knit on WS
●	MB
✕	Left Twist
✕	Right Twist

SCHEMATIC

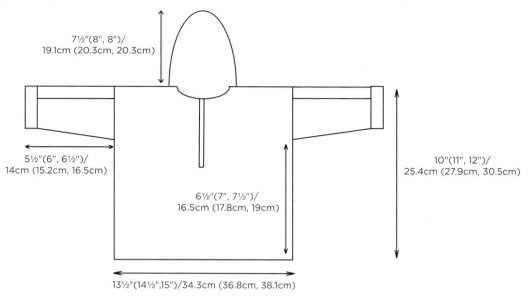

7½"(8", 8")/
19.1cm (20.3cm, 20.3cm)

5½"(6", 6½")/
14cm (15.2cm, 16.5cm)

10"(11", 12")/
25.4cm (27.9cm, 30.5cm)

6½"(7", 7½")/
16.5cm (17.8cm, 19cm)

13½"(14½",15")/34.3cm (36.8cm, 38.1cm)

cast-on st. Slip 6th, 5th, 4th, 3rd, 2nd, and first st over cast-on st, leaving 1 loop. Cut yarn leaving 2"/5.1cm tail. Thread tail through loop to secure. Knot yarn tails together tightly to secure button.

I-Cord Edging for Button Loops (Make 4)

Work on Left Front opening edge for boys, Right Front for girls.

CO 2 sts, leaving 2"/5cm yarn tail. Work in I-cord for 5 rows. Do not cut yarn. Slip 2 sts onto stitch holder. Thread end of 2"/5cm yarn tail through edge of front opening at bottom and secure. *[Slip 2 sts back onto needles, then with 2nd needle, slip 2nd stitch over the first st and off the needle, leaving 1 st on needles. Slip tip of same needle into the edge of opening 1"/2.5cm from the previous attachment point of I-cord. Pick up and knit 1 st (2 sts on needle). Work in I-cord for 5 rows]; rep from * 3 more times, making sure loops are evenly spaced along neck edge.

FINISHING AND ASSEMBLY

1. Weave in ends.
2. Sew sleeve seams and 1"/2.5cm of side seams at underarms.
3. Make bobble buttons and I-cord edging according to instructions. Place buttons opposite I-cord loops on front opening.
4. Place buttons over Right Front opening edge for boys and Left Front opening edge for girls. Thread yarn tails from front of work to back, knot, and weave in ends.

DESIGN TIP

For a more streamlined look, substitute a zipper for the buttons.

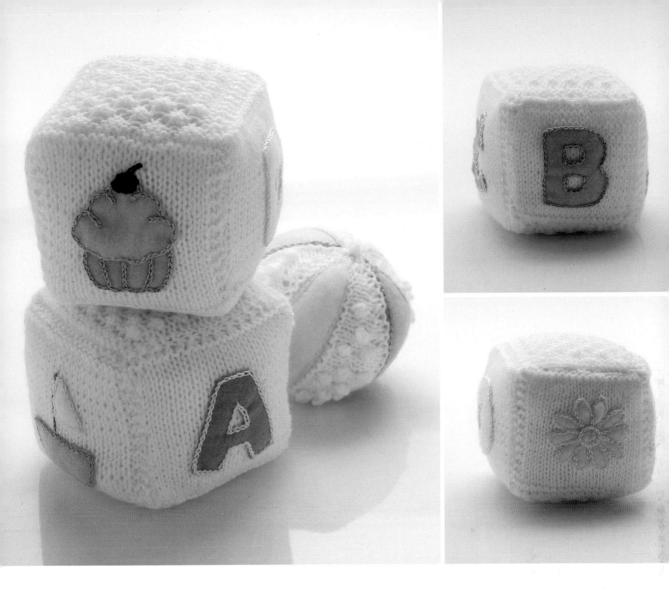

A-IS-FOR-ADORABLE
BLOCKS AND BALL

And *b* is for *baby*, which means these knitted blocks and ball are the perfect gift for a mom-to-be or the new arrival. Soft bramble and bobble stitch textures and felted appliqués create beautiful heirloom-quality toys.

SKILL LEVEL
Easy

FINISHED MEASUREMENTS
Block:
Height: 4"/10cm
Width: 4"/10cm
Depth: 4"/10cm

Ball:
Circumference: 13"/33cm

YARN
1 skein of Lion Brand Yarns Babysoft (60% acrylic/40% nylon), 5 oz/140g = 459 yd/420m per skein) in color #157 pale yellow OR approximately 459 yd/420m lightweight acrylic/nylon blend yarn in pale yellow

MATERIALS
- Size 6 U.S. (4mm) needles, or size needed to obtain gauge
- Tapestry needle
- Stitch markers
- 1 bag of Poly-fil (100% polyester fiberfill, 12 oz) OR one 12-oz bag of polyester fiberfill
- 1 9" x 12" (23 x 31cm) sheet each of Kunin Rainbow Classicfelt in Baby Blue (#660), Baby Pink (#0530), Cashmere Tan (#884), White (#550), and Yellow (#351) OR one 9 x 12" (23 x 31cm) sheet of felt in light blue, light pink, tan, white, and yellow

- Scissors
- Sewing needle
- Thread to match lining fabric
- 1 skein DMC pearl cotton size 5 (100% cotton, 27.3 yd/25m) each in Ultra Very Lt. Tan (#739), Lt. Pale Yellow (#745), Medium Pink (#776), Very Lt. Beige Brown (#842), Lt. Baby Blue (#3325), and Red (#321) OR approximately 27.3 yd/25m size 5 cotton embroidery thread in light tan, pale yellow, pink, light beige brown, and light blue
- ¼ yd (23cm) muslin or lightweight cotton fabric of your choice

GAUGE
22 sts and 26 rows = 4"/10cm over St st
Always take time to check your gauge.

PATTERN NOTES
- The blocks are knitted flat. Stitches are picked up separately along 2 edges of the first panel.
- The ball is formed by knitting short rows.
- Both chart and written instructions for Bramble Stitch are provided. Choose the instruction method you prefer.
- Letters, side strips (ball), and objects are cut from templates. The felted pieces are chain-stitched to the blocks and ball as shown in the templates. (Refer to cutting and Stitching Diagram.) A lining is sewn for each item, stuffed with polyester fiberfill, and placed inside each knitted block and ball. Finally, the seams are hand-stitched closed.
- For instructions on chain stitch, see page 36.
- For instructions on whipstitching, see page 36.

SPECIAL ABBREVIATIONS
Make Bobble (MB): [K1, p1, k1, p1, k1, p1, k1] into next st, making 7 sts from one; then pass 6th, 5th, 4th, 3rd, 2nd, and first st over the last st made.
P3tog: Purl 3 sts together.

STITCH PATTERNS
Stockinette Stitch (St st)
Row 1: Knit.
Row 2: Purl.
Rep Rows 1–2 for Stockinette Stitch patt.

Bramble Stitch (over a multiple of 4 sts + 2)
Row 1: Purl.
Row 2: K1, *p3tog, [k1, p1, k1] into next st; rep from * to last st, k1.
Row 3: Purl.
Row 4: K1, *[k1, p1, k1] into next st, p3tog; rep from * to last st, k1.
Rep Rows 1–4 for Bramble Stitch patt.

Blocks (Make 2)

CO 20 sts.

Knit 2 rows.

Row 3 (WS): K2, purl across to last 2 sts, k2.

Row 4 (RS): K2, knit across to last 2 sts, k2.

Rep Rows 3 and 4 for 23 more rows, ending with a RS row.

Rows 27, 28, and 29: Knit across.

Row 30 (RS): K2, work Row 1 of Bramble Stitch patt to last 2 sts, k2.

Row 31 (WS): K2, work Row 2 of Bramble St patt to last 2 sts, k2.

Work in patt as established for 22 more rows.

Rows 54–56: Knit .

Rep Rows 3–55 once more. BO all sts.

Pick up 20 sts from side of first bramble block and knit in St st until 24 rows are completed. BO all sts.

Pick up 20 sts from other side of same bramble block and knit in St st until 24 rows are completed. BO all sts.

BALL

CO 28 sts.

Knit 1 row.

Row 1 (WS): Sl 1, purl to last st. Turn (1 st on RH needle).

Row 2: Sl 1, knit to last 2 sts. Turn.

Row 3: Sl 1, purl to last 3 sts. Turn.

Row 4: Sl 1, knit to last 4 sts. Turn.

Row 5: Sl 1, purl to last 5 sts. Turn.

Row 6: Sl 1, knit to last 6 sts. Turn.

Row 7: Sl 1, purl to last 7 sts. Turn.

Row 8: Sl 1, knit to last 8 sts. Turn.

Row 9: Sl 1, purl to last 9 sts. Turn

Row 10: Sl 1, knit to last 8 sts, * with RH needle pick up horizontal bar, knit next st, slip horizontal bar over the knit st and off RH needle, k1; rep from * 3 more times, k1.

Row 11: Knit across to last 9 sts, * with RH needle pick up horizontal bar, knit next st, slip horizontal bar over the knit st and off RH needle, k1; rep from * 3 more times, k1.

Row 12: Knit.

Row 13: Sl 1, purl to last st. Turn.

Row 14: Sl 1, *k3, MB; rep from * to last 6 sts, k4. Turn.

Row 15: Sl 1, purl to last 3 sts. Turn.

Row 16: Sl 1, *k3, MB; rep from * to last 8 sts, k4. Turn.

Row 17: Sl 1, purl to last 5 sts. Turn.

Row 18: Sl 1, *k3, MB; rep from * to last 10 sts, k4. Turn.

Row 19: Sl 1, purl to last 7 sts. Turn.

Row 20: Sl 1, *k3, MB; rep from * to last 12 sts, k4. Turn.

Row 21: Sl 1, purl to last 9 sts. Turn.

Row 22: Sl 1, knit to last 8 sts, * with RH needle pick up horizontal bar, knit next st, slip horizontal bar over the knit st and off RH needle, k1; rep from * 3 more times, k1.

Row 23: Knit across to last 9 sts, * with RH needle pick up horizontal bar, knit next st, slip horizontal bar over the knit st and off RH needle, k1; rep from * 3 more times, k1.

Rep Rows 1–23 3 more times.

Next Row: Knit.

BO all sts.

FINISHING AND ASSEMBLY

1. Weave in ends.
2. Cut felt for both blocks and ball according to templates.
3. Center cutouts on St st area on each square or side of ball. Pin in place.
4. Using Stitching Diagram as guide, chain-stitch over felted letters and objects with colors indicated.

STITCH CHART
**Bramble Stitch
(multiple of 4 sts +2)**

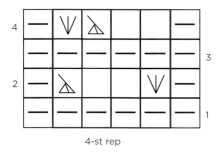

4-st rep

Legend

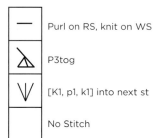

| — | Purl on RS, knit on WS |
| P3tog |
| [K1, p1, k1] into next st |
| No Stitch |

CUTTING DIAGRAM
Felt Strips for Ball

Side Strips for Ball
(Cut 2 in white,1 in light blue,
and 1 in light pink felt)

1½"/3.8cm   5½"/12.7cm

---

5. Cut out lining for blocks and ball, adding ¼"(0.6cm) seam allowance to measurements of knitted pieces around all edges. Sew sides of lining, leaving one area unstitched for insertion of stuffing. Turn RS out through opening. Stuff lining with polyester fiberfill.

6. With matching cotton thread, close the opening by whipstitching.

7. Place stuffed block or ball in knitted cover and whipstitch around the sides to enclose.

8. Weave in loose ends.

DESIGN TIP
Use leftover yarn to make blocks for additional letters, including the baby's initials.

CUTTING AND STITCHING DIAGRAM
Felt Appliqués for Blocks

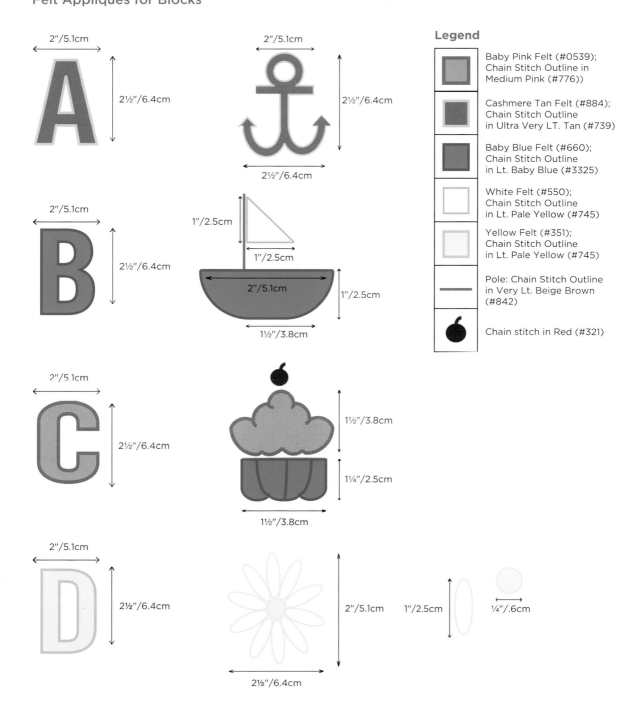

Legend

	Baby Pink Felt (#0539); Chain Stitch Outline in Medium Pink (#776))
	Cashmere Tan Felt (#884); Chain Stitch Outline in Ultra Very LT. Tan (#739)
	Baby Blue Felt (#660); Chain Stitch Outline in Lt. Baby Blue (#3325)
	White Felt (#550); Chain Stitch Outline in Lt. Pale Yellow (#745)
	Yellow Felt (#351); Chain Stitch Outline in Lt. Pale Yellow (#745)
	Pole: Chain Stitch Outline in Very Lt. Beige Brown (#842)
	Chain stitch in Red (#321)

DOME AFGHAN

Inspired by the architecture of the brilliant domes of Córdoba, Spain, this afghan is knit outward from a central star diamond. The piece is knitted in the round and grows, round by round, resulting in a beautifully constructed geometric shape.

SKILL LEVEL
Intermediate

FINISHED MEASUREMENTS
Diameter at widest point: 35"/89cm

YARN
1 skein of Briar Rose Fibers Celebration (60% merino wool/40% bamboo, 8 oz/226g = 600 yd/548m per skein) in color 3010 Coral and Golds OR approximately 600 yd/548m medium-weight wool yarn in coral-gold multi

MATERIALS
- Size 6 U.S. (4mm) double-pointed and circular needles, or size needed to obtain gauge
- Stitch markers
- Tapestry needle
- Crochet hook for attaching fringe
- 7" (17.8cm)-wide cardboard strip for making fringe

GAUGE
20 sts = 4"/10cm over St st Always take time to check your gauge.

PATTERN NOTES
- The afghan is knitted in the round. Begin with double-pointed needles and change to a circular needle when necessary to accommodate stitches.
- Only chart instructions for Dome Lace Stitch are provided.
- The charts can be enlarged for ease of use.
- Place a stitch marker between repeats of Dome Lace Stitch pattern to assist in counting. Use a unique marker to designate beginning of round.
- Work Dome Lace Stitch 6 times around.

SPECIAL ABBREVIATIONS
Skp: Slip 1 st, knit next st. Pass the slipped st over the knit st and off the needle.
Sk2p: Slip 1 st, knit 2 sts together. Pass the slipped st over the knit st and off the needle.
K2tog: Knit 2 sts together.
Yo: Yarn over.
M1R: Insert LH needle from back to front into the horizontal strand between the last st worked and the next st on LH needle. Pick up this strand and knit through the front loop. This will twist the newly formed st.
M1L: Insert LH needle from front to back into the horizontal strand between the last st worked and the next st on LH needle. Pick up this strand and knit through the back loop. This will twist the newly formed st.
K1tbl: Knit 1 st through back loop.

Inc 2: Increase by knitting into front, back, and then front of the same st before slipping it off the needle.

AFGHAN
Using dpns (or circular needle), CO 18 sts. Divide onto 3 or 4 dpns, pm for beg of rnd, and join, being careful not to twist sts. Begin Dome Lace Stitch patt, placing markers between patt rep. Work Rows 1–112 once, working patt 6 times around afghan. Change to longer circular needle when necessary. BO all sts.

FINISHING AND ASSEMBLY
Weave in ends. Stretch and block afghan.

FRINGE
(Make 11)
The general instructions for making fringe are on page 31. Wrap the yarn around the width of the cardboard strip 9 times. Use crochet hook to attach fringe at each point of star. Trim ends evenly.

DESIGN TIP
You can embellish this afghan with a crocheted edging instead of fringe.

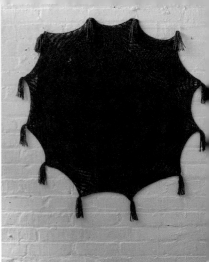

STITCH CHART
Dome Lace Stitch

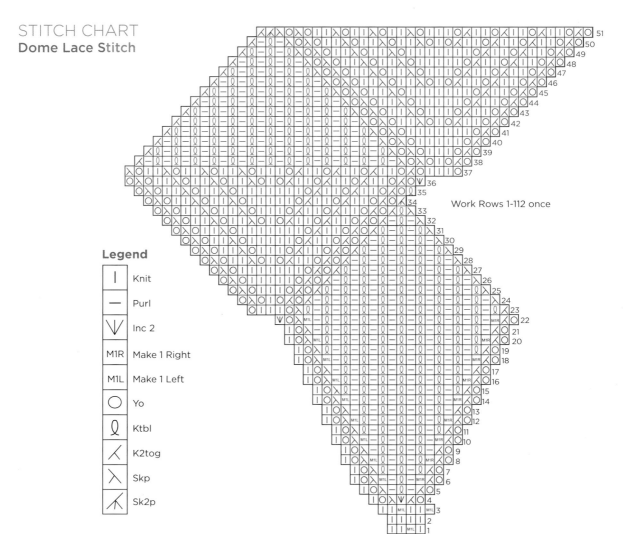

Work Rows 1-112 once

Legend

I	Knit
—	Purl
V	Inc 2
M1R	Make 1 Right
M1L	Make 1 Left
O	Yo
Q	Ktbl
⋏	K2tog
⋋	Skp
⋀	Sk2p

Work patt six times around

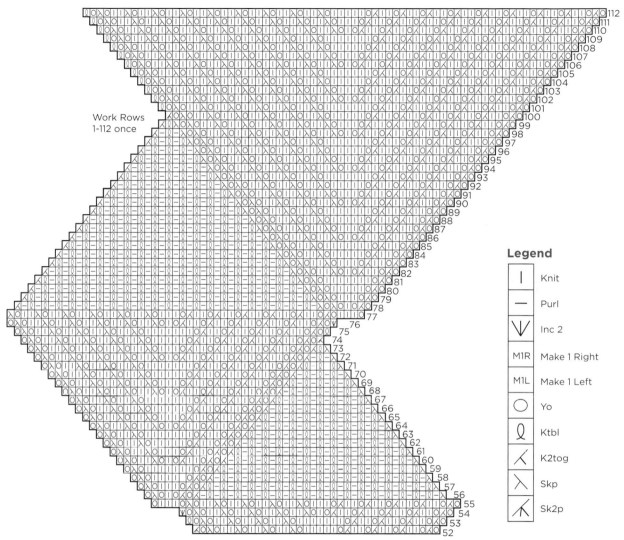

Work Rows
1-112 once

Work patt six times around

Legend

I	Knit
—	Purl
V	Inc 2
M1R	Make 1 Right
M1L	Make 1 Left
O	Yo
Q	Ktbl
⟋	K2tog
⟍	Skp
⋏	Sk2p

STEP-FORWARD KNEE-HIGH SOCKS

Socks are a classic knitted gift, and these go the extra mile—they're long enough to reach just over the knee. Knit from toe up and including lace patterns and an eye-of-partridge heel, this pair is the perfect gift for the sock lover in your life.

SKILL LEVEL
Intermediate

SIZE
One size: fits women's shoe sizes U.S. 6–8½

FINISHED MEASUREMENTS
Length: 22"/56cm from cuff to heel
Approx 9½"/24.1cm from heel to toe

YARN
1 skein of Dream in Color Baby (100% Superfine Australian Merino, 4 oz/113g = 700 yd/640m per skein) in color #VS11 Cinnamon Girl OR approximately 700 yd/640m super fine–weight mohair yarn in orange-brown

MATERIALS
- Size 3 U.S. (3.25mm) double-pointed or circular needles, or size to obtain gauge
- Stitch marker
- Tapestry needle
- Small amount of scrap yarn for provisional cast-on

GAUGE
28 sts and 36 rows = 4"/10cm in St st
Always take time to check your gauge.

PATTERN NOTES
- Both chart and written instructions are provided for the Step-Forward Lace Stitch (Chart A) and Step-Forward Calf Lace Stitch (Chart B). Choose the instruction method you prefer.
- For instructions on Knit Wrap (KW), refer to pages 29–30.
- For instructions on Purl Wrap (PW), refer to pages 29–30.
- For instructions on provisional cast-on, refer to page 19.
- Gusset instructions are provided for both narrow and wide feet.
- These socks are knit in the round except for toe and heel sections, which require turning the work to create short rows.
- When working Step-Forward Lace Stitch and Step-Forward Calf Lace Stitch pattern from chart, read all rounds from right to left.
- Use scrap yarn in a similar weight and contrasting color for provisional cast-on.

SPECIAL ABBREVIATIONS
Sk2p: Slip 1 st, knit 2 sts together. Pass the slipped st over the knit st and off the needle.
K3tog: Knit 3 sts together.
KW: Knit wrap.
PW: Purl wrap.
KDW: Pick up double-wrapped st with knit st, knit together.
PDW: Pick up double-wrapped st with purl st, purl together.
M1R: Insert LH needle from back to front into the horizontal strand between the last st worked and the next st on LH needle. Pick up this strand and knit through the front loop. This will twist the newly formed st.
M1L: Insert LH needle from front to back into the horizontal strand between the last st worked and the next st on LH needle. Pick up this strand and knit through the back loop. This will twist the newly formed st.
K1tbl: Knit 1 through back loop.
Sl 1: Slip 1 st.
Skp: Slip 1 st, knit the next st. Pass the slipped st over knit st and off the needle.

STITCH PATTERNS
Step-Forward Lace Stitch (over 27 sts)
Rnd 1: K1, (k2tog, yo) 2 times, p2, k2tog, p2, k2, yo, p1, yo, k2, p2, skp, p2, (yo, skp) 2 times, k1.
Rnd 2: (K2tog, yo) 2 times, p2, k2tog, p2, k2, yo, k1tbl, p1, k1tbl, yo, k2, p2, skp, p2, (yo, skp) 2 times.
Rnd 3: K1, k2tog, yo, p2, k2tog, p2, k2, yo, (p1, k1tbl) 2 times, p1, yo, k2, p2, skp, p2, yo, skp, k1.
Rnd 4: K2tog, yo, p2, k2tog, p2, k2, yo, (k1tbl, p1) 3 times,

k1tbl, yo, k2, p2, skp, p2, yo, skp.

Rnd 5: K1, p2, k2tog, p2, k2, yo, (p1, k1tbl) 4 times, p1, yo, k2, p2, skp, p2, k1.

Rnd 6: P2, k2tog, p2, k2, yo, (k1tbl, p1) 5 times, k1tbl, yo, k2, p2, skp, p2.

Rnd 7: P1, K2tog, p2, k2, yo, (p1, k1tbl) 6 times, p1, yo, k2, p2, skp, p1.

Rnd 8: K2tog, p2, k2, yo, (k1tbl, p1) 7 times, k1tbl, yo, k2, p2, skp.

Rep Rnds 1–8 for Step-Forward Lace Stitch patt.

Step-Forward Calf Lace Stitch (over 53 sts)

Rnd 1: K1, *(k2tog, yo) 2 times, p2, k2tog, p2, k2, yo, p1, yo, k2, p2, skp, p2, (yo, skp) 2 times*, k1; rep from * to * once more, k1.

Rnd 2: (K2tog, yo) 2 times, p2, k2tog, *p2, k2, yo, k1tbl, p1, k1tbl, yo, k2, p2, skp, p2*, yo, skp, yo, sk2p, yo, k2tog, yo, p2, k2tog; rep from * to * once more, (yo, skp) 2 times.

Rnd 3: K1, *k2tog, yo, p2, k2tog, p2, k2, yo, (p1, k1tbl) 2 times, p1, yo, k2, p2, skp, p2, yo, skp*, k1; rep from * to * once more, k1.

Rnd 4: K2tog, *yo, p2, k2tog, p2, k2, yo, (k1tbl, p1) 3 times, k1tbl, yo, k2, p2, skp, p2, yo*, sk2p; rep from * to * one more, skp.

Rnd 5: K1, *p2, k2tog, p2, k2, yo, (p1, k1tbl) 4 times, p1, yo, k2, p2, skp, p2*, k1; rep from * to * once more, k1.

Rnd 6: P2, *k2tog, p2, k2, yo, (k1tbl, p1) 5 times, k1tbl, yo, k2, p2, skp*, p3; rep from * to * once more, p2.

Rnd 7: P1, *k2tog, p2, k2, yo, (p1, k1tbl) 6 times, p1, yo, k2, p2, skp*, p1; rep from * to * once more, p1.

Rnd 8: K2tog, *p2, k2, yo, (k1tbl, p1) 7 times, k1tbl, yo, k2, p2*, sk2p; rep from * to * once more, skp.

Rep Rounds 1–8 for Step-Forward Calf Lace Stitch patt.

Sock (Make 2)
Toe

Using scrap yarn and provisional cast-on CO 27 sts.

With sock yarn, begin toe.

Row 1 (WS): Purl to end. Turn work.

Row 2 (RS): K25, KW next st. Turn work.

Row 3 (WS): P23, PW next st. Turn work.

Row 4: K22, KW next st. Turn work.

Row 5: P21, PW next st. Turn work.

Row 6: K20, KW next st. Turn work.

Row 7: P19, PW next st. Turn work.

Row 8: K18, KW next st. Turn work.

Row 9: P17, PW next st. Turn work.

Row 10: K16, KW next st. Turn work.

Row 11: P15, PW next stitch. Turn work.

Row 12: K14, KW next st. Turn work.

Row 13: P13, PW next st. Turn work.

Row 14: K12, KW next st. Turn work.

Row 15: P11, PW next st. Turn work.

Picking Up Wrapped Stitches on Toe

Row 16: Knit across to next wrapped st, knit next st together with wrapped st, KW next st (2 wraps on st). Turn work.

Row 17: Purl across to next wrapped st, purl next st with wrapped st, PW next st (2 wraps on st). Turn work.

Row 18: Knit across to next double-wrapped st, KDW, KW next st. Turn work.

Row 19: Purl across to next double-wrapped st, PDW, PW next st. Turn work.

Rep Rows 18 and 19 until both end sts have been wrapped.

Next Row: Knit across to next wrapped st, knit with wrapped st.

Next Row: Purl across to last purled st, purl with wrapped st.

Next Row: Knit across.

FOOT
Arranging Stitches

Remove waste yarn from provisional cast-on (see page 19) and place 27 sts on needle as waste yarn is being removed (pick up an extra st if necessary) (54 sts). Knit across 27 sts, pm; end of instep sts. K27, pm; end of sole sts. Arrange sts on dpns. Foot will now be worked in the rnd.

Next Rnd: Work instep sts in Step Forward Lace Stitch (Chart A), and knit across sole sts.

Work in the rnd in patt as established until foot measures 7"/18cm, or to 2"/5cm less than desired length. Complete instep sts.

Short Gusset (Narrow Feet)

Rnd 1: K1, M1R, knit across to last st before marker, M1L, k1. Work instep sts in Step-Forward Lace Stitch patt (Chart A).

Rep Rnd 1 for 14 rnds, until there is a total of 82 sts, ending with instep sts.

Next Rnd: Keeping markers at each end of instep sts, knit next 14 sole sts. Slip 14 sts from the other side of sole to instep section (27 sole sts, 14 gusset sts, 27 instep sts, 14 gusset sts). Separate gusset sts from instep sts with markers.

Gusset (Wide Feet)

Rnd 1: K1, M1R, knit across to last st before marker, M1L, k1. Work instep sts in Step-Forward Lace Stitch patt (Chart A).

Rnd 2: Knit across sole sts to last 27 sts. Work instep sts. Rep Rnds 1 and 2 for 28 rnds (14 times), until there is a total of 82 sts, ending with instep sts.

Next Rnd: Keeping markers at each end of instep sts, knit next 14 sole sts. Slip 14 sts from the other side of sole to instep section (27 sole sts, 14 gusset sts, 27 instep sts, 14 gusset sts). Separate gusset sts from instep sts with markers.

Short-Row Heel (over 27 sole sts)

Row 1 (RS): K25, KW next st. Turn work.
Row 2 (WS): P23, PW next st. Turn work.
Row 3: K22, KW next st. Turn work.
Row 4: P21, PW next st. Turn work.
Row 5: K20, KW next st. Turn work.
Row 6: P19, PW next st. Turn work.
Row 7: K18, KW next st. Turn work.
Row 8: P17, PW next st. Turn work.
Row 9: K16, KW next st. Turn work.

Row 10: P15, PW next st. Turn work.
Row 11: K14 sts, KW next stitch. Turn work.
Row 12: Purl across to last st, pick up wraps and purl together with sts. Purl the last st together with first st from gusset. Turn work.
Row 13: Knit across to last st, pick up wraps and knit together with sts. Knit the last st together with the first st from gusset. Turn work.
Row 14: Slip 1 purlwise. Purl to last st. Purl last st together with next st from gusset.

Eye-of-Partridge Heel

Row 1 (RS): Slip 1 purlwise, k1, M1R, *k1, sl 1 purlwise; rep from * to last st, knit last st together with next gusset st.
Row 2 (WS): Slip 1 st purlwise, purl to last st, purl last st together with next gusset st.
Row 3: Sl 1 st purlwise, *sl 1 purlwise, k1; rep from * to last 2 sts, k1, knit next st together with next gusset st.
Row 4: Rep Row 2.
Row 5: Slip 1 st purlwise, *k1, sl 1 st purlwise; rep from * to last st, knit last st together with next gusset st.

Rep Rows 2–5 until all gusset sts are worked.

Last Row: *Sl 1 st purlwise, k1; rep from * to last 3 sts, knit last 2 sts together with next gusset st. Join rnd, and work across instep sts (54 sts).

Leg Shaping

Inc Rnd: K1, M1R, knit across back of leg to last st before instep sts, M1L, k1. Work across instep sts.
Next Rnd: Knit across back of

STITCH CHARTS

Legend

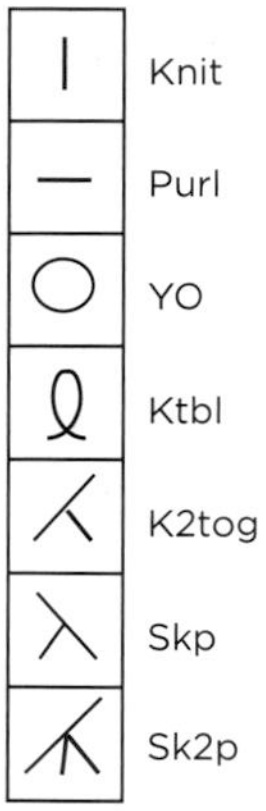
Knit
Purl
YO
Ktbl
K2tog
Skp
Sk2p

Step-Forward Lace Stitch (Chart A)
(over 27 sts)

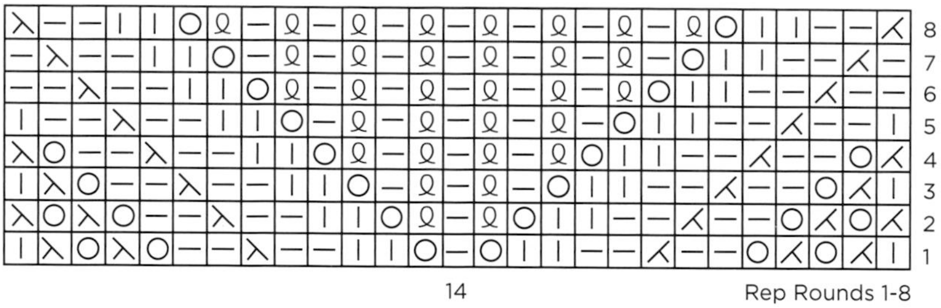
8
7
6
5
4
3
2
1
14
Rep Rounds 1-8

Step-Forward Calf Lace Stitch (Chart B)
(over 53 sts)

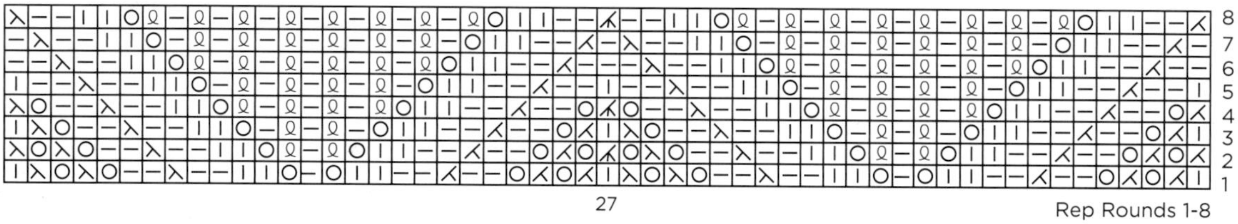
8
7
6
5
4
3
2
1
27
Rep Rounds 1-8

leg, work across instep sts. Cont in patt as established, rep Increase Rnd every 6th rnd 10 more times, then every 5 rnds 2 times (80 sts).

Calf Shaping

Next Rnd: Work Step-Forward Calf Lace Stitch patt (Chart B) over next 53 sts, work instep sts. Cont working calf and instep sts as established until calf measures 8"/20.3cm or 4"/10cm less than desired height of knee-high sock. End with Rnd 8 of Step-Forward Calf Lace Stitch.

Cuff

Rnd 1: K1, sl previous st over knit st, (p1, k1tbl) 12 times, purl, k2tog, (p1, k1tbl) 25 times, p1, pm to indicate end of rnd.

Rnd 2: *K1tbl, p1; rep from * around.

Rep Rnd 2 until cuff measures 4"/10cm. BO.

FINISHING AND ASSEMBLY

1. Weave in ends, closing holes.
2. Work 2nd sock.

DESIGN TIP

For added support, knit the cuff section with an extra-thin beading elastic along with the yarn.

EMERALD LAPTOP CASE

This laptop case is the perfect gift for someone who's bored with the same old black briefcase. Knit with jeweltone variegated yarn, this bag is felted and embellished with stylish embroidery. Fully lined pockets and a foam interior provide all the protection of a classic laptop case. This one-ball project is just the thing to pamper a special friend.

SKILL LEVEL
Easy

FINISHED MEASUREMENTS
Length: 13"/33cm
Width: 17¾"/44.5cm
Depth: 1½"/3.8cm

YARN
1 hank of Briar Rose Fiber Abundance (100% Corriedale wool, 16 oz./456g = 750 yd/685m per hank) in color #8197 OR approximately 750 yd/685m worsted-weight wool yarn in bright olive and medium blues and greens

MATERIALS
- Size 7 U.S. (4.5mm) needles or size to obtain gauge
- 20" (51cm) heavy-duty zipper in green
- 1 package BagWorks ⅝" gold snaps, #A3117-GLD, OR two ⅝" (1.6cm) snaps in gold
- 1 package Dritz ¾" (1.9cm) gold purse handle loops, #9843, OR two ¾" (1.9cm) purse handle loops in gold
- ½ yd (46cm) of ½" (1.27cm)–wide foam
- Straight pins
- Stitch marker
- Tapestry needle
- ¼ yd (23cm) nylon lining fabric of your choice
- Cotton thread to match lining
- Sewing needle
- Hammer (for applying snaps)
- Two 1 x ¾" (2.5 x 1.9cm) Velcro spots or circles

GAUGE
14 sts = 4"/10cm over St st
Always take time to check your gauge.

PATTERN NOTES
- The knitted pieces are felted, cut according to Cutting Template specifications, and hand- or machine-sewn together.
- For bag construction, refer to the Finishing and Assembly instructions and accompanying Construction Diagram.
- Foam can be purchased at your local fabric store in the upholstery section or where pillow stuffing is sold.
- For instructions on felting, see page 33.
- For instructions on whipstitching, see page 36.
- For instructions on Lazy Daisy Stitch, see page 36.
- For instructions on inserting zipper, see page 37.

STITCH PATTERN
Stockinette Stitch (St st)
Row 1: Knit.
Row 2: Purl.
Rep Rows 1–2 for Stockinette Stitch patt.

LAPTOP CASE
Body
CO 84 sts. Work in St st until piece measures 33"/83.8cm. BO.

Flap
CO 84 sts. Work in St st until piece measures 18"/45.7cm. BO.

Side Edge
CO 13 sts. Work in St st until piece measures 57"/145cm. BO.

Handle
CO 13 sts. Work in St st until piece measures 40"/101.6cm. BO.

FELTING
Felt the knitted pieces. Check to make sure the Body does not shrink beyond the final dimensions shown in the Cutting Template. (Note that the Body will be cut in 2.) Lay pieces flat to air-dry.

FINISHING AND ASSEMBLY
1. Cut Body into 2 pieces as shown in the Cutting Template.
2. Cut Flap, Side Edge, and Handle according to measurements in Cutting Template.
3. Embroider Lazy Daisy Stitch on bottom (curved) edges of Flap as shown in Cutting Template.
4. Cut linings from chosen fabric for all pieces as follows, adding ¼"/0.6cm extra around all edges for seam allowance:

- Cut 2 linings for Side Edge, each 2"/5.1cm shorter than felted edge piece. This will leave 1"/2.5cm of extra felt on each end to form a tab.
- Cut 4 linings for Body.
- Cut 1 lining each for Flap and Handle.

5. Place ball side of gold snap closures 1"/2.5cm from bottom and 1¾"/3.8cm from sides of curved edge of flap lining (1 on each side of bag). Attach according to manufacturer's directions.

6. Machine- or hand-sew linings to felted Flap and Handle, turning in extra ¼"/0.6cm on all edges.

7. Cut 2 foam pieces, each 11½"/29.2cm high, using Body as template. Foam is 2"/5.1cm shorter than felted Body.

8. Sew felted bag back and front to Side Edge, allowing 1"/2.5cm of Side Edge to extend, unsewn, beyond top of bag at both sides. Hand- or machine-stitch securely on the WS of fabric.

9. Pin lined side of Flap 4"/10cm down from top edge of felt back. Whipstitch in place.

10. Fold Flap over felted Body front and mark position where snaps fall on front.

11. Place socket side of snap closure on front. Attach according to

manufacturer's directions.

12. Fold 1"/2.5cm felt extension of Side Edge over purse handle loop. Fold edge to inside of bag; whipstitch to secure. Repeat for other side.

13. Cut out linings for both pieces of foam, using foam as template.

14. Sew linings for foam around 3 sides, keeping top edge open to form a pocket. Place 1 foam piece inside of lining pocket. Whipstitch closed.

15. Place lined foam on top of 1 body lining, matching side edges. Sew together around 3 sides, leaving top edge unsewn.

16. Sew the 2nd body lining to side edge lining.

17. Sew WS of side edge lining to the foam body piece, placing lined foam between 2 sides of body lining.

18. Cut 2 x 6"/5 x 15.2cm tab from lining material for closure inside of bag. Fold lengthwise and sew 3 remaining sides, keeping 2"/5cm opening on long side. Turn RS out. Whipstitch opening closed. Iron tab.

19. Center one edge of tab 4"/10cm from top edge of back (inside bag). Sew across top edge of tab.

20. Lay open side of tab onto the lined foam, mark for Velcro placement.

21. Place fuzzy side of Velcro on bottom of tab edge. Place hard side of Velcro on front of lined foam.

22. For remaining linings, attach both body pieces to side edge, forming 2nd body lining. Do not sew in other foam piece.

23. Place Body lined with foam inside of 2nd body lining with WS facing each other.

24. Whipstitch top edges of all body linings together by tucking raw edges between linings.

25. Place lining inside of bag.

26. Place unlined foam piece between felted Body and the side where the lined Body is attached to the foam pocket. Unlined foam should now lie between lining and felted Body.

27. Pin zipper around top edges of Body. Whipstitch zipper enclosure to top of edges. **Note:** Zipper enclosure will extend along the length of the Body.

28. Tuck extended zipper between felted sides and lining.

29. Whipstitch lining to inside of zipper edge.

30. Pull edges of lined, felted Handle through purse handle loops. Whipstitch 2"/5cm inward from the edges to lined side of Handle. Secure in place.

CUTTING TEMPLATE

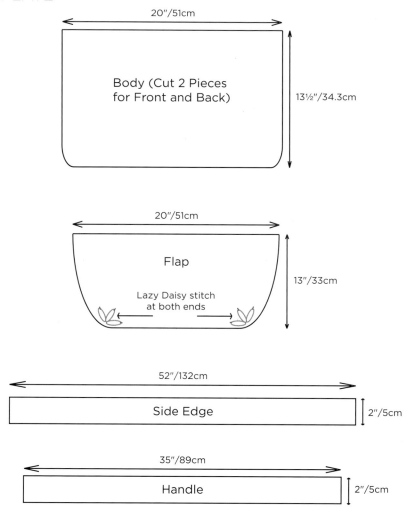

20"/51cm

Body (Cut 2 Pieces
for Front and Back)

13½"/34.3cm

20"/51cm

Flap

Lazy Daisy stitch
at both ends

13"/33cm

52"/132cm

Side Edge

2"/5cm

35"/89cm

Handle

2"/5cm

DESIGN TIP

If you don't want to use
nylon for the lining, choose
another waterproof fabric that
will protect your laptop, such
as taffeta.

CONSTRUCTION DIAGRAM

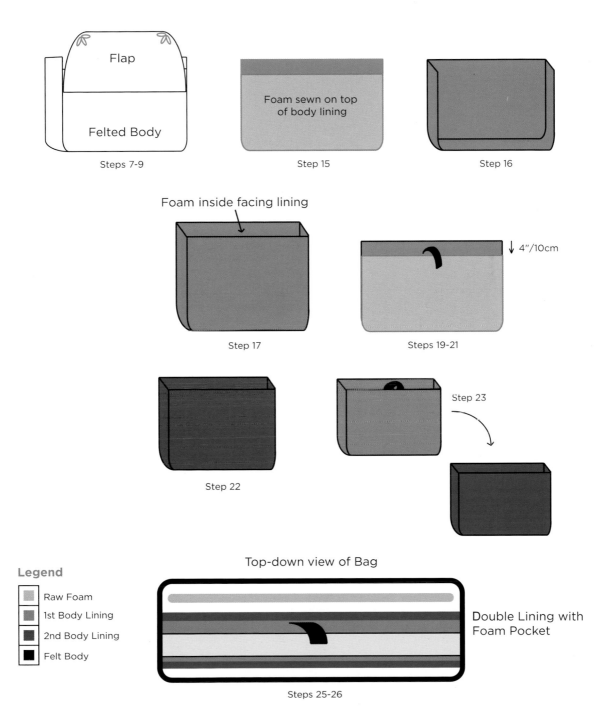

Flap

Felted Body

Steps 7-9

Foam sewn on top of body lining

Step 15

Step 16

Foam inside facing lining

Step 17

↓ 4"/10cm

Steps 19-21

Step 22

Step 23

Legend

Raw Foam
1st Body Lining
2nd Body Lining
Felt Body

Top-down view of Bag

Double Lining with Foam Pocket

Steps 25-26

SUPPLIERS

YARN

Bernat and Patons Yarns
Distributed by
Spinrite LP
320 Livingstone Avenue South
Listowel, ON
Canada N4W 3H3
888-368-8401
www.bernat.com

Berroco, Inc.
14 Elmdale Road
P.O. Box 367
Uxbridge, MA 01569
www.Berroco.com

Blue Sky Alpacas, Inc
P.O. Box 88
Cedar, MN 55011
888-460-8862
www.blueskyalpacas.com

Briar Rose Fibers
chris@briarrosefibers.net
616-554-4900
www.briarrosefibers.net

Brown Sheep Co., Inc.
100662 County Road 16
Mitchell, NE 69357
800-826-9136
www.brownsheep.com

Crystal Palace Yarns
Distributed by
Straw into Gold, Inc.
160 23rd Street
Richard, CA 94804
www.straw.com

Dream in Color Yarn
dream@dreamincoloryarn.com
www.dreamincoloryarn.com

Kollage Yarns
3304 Blue Bell Lane
Birmingham, AL 35242
888-829-7758
www.kollageyarns.com

Lion Brand Yarns
135 Kero Road
Carlstadt, NJ 07072
800-258-YARN
www.lionbrand.com

Louet North America
3425 Hands Rd,
Prescott, ON, Canada
K0E 1T0
Phone: 613-925-4502
Fax: 613-925-1405
www.louet.com

Mountain Colors
P.O. Box 156
Corvallis, MT 59828
406-961-1900
www.mountaincolors.com

Noro Yarns
Distributed by
Knitting Fever Inc.
P.O. Box 336
315 Bayview Avenue
Amityville, NY 11701
516-546-3600
www.knittingfever.com

Skacel Collection, Inc.
800-255-1278
info@skacelknitting.com

South West Trading Company
www.soysilk.com

Filatura Di Crosa
Distributed by
Tahki Stacy Charles, Inc.
70-30 80th St., Bldg 36
Ridgewood, NY 11385
800-338-YARN
www.tahkistacycharles.com

FABRIC AND LEATHER

Clifton Associates Inc.
1000 Main Ave.
Clifton, NJ 07011
800-USA-PILE
www.big4fabrics.com

Leather Cord USA
503 Hickory Ridge Trail
Suite 110
Woodstock, GA 30188
877-700-CORD
www.LeatherCordUSA.com

Tandy Leather Factory, Inc
3847 East Loop 820 South
Fort Worth, TX 76119
800-433-3201
www.tandyleatherfactory.com

PURSE HARDWARE

BagWorks Inc.
Attn: Customer Service
3301-C South
Cravens Road
Fort Worth, TX 76119
800-365-7423
www.bagworks.com

Dritz
Distributed by
Prym Consumer USA Inc.
P.O. Box 5028
Spartanburg, SC 29304
800-255-7696
www.dritz.com

INDEX